Chloe's Vegan Kitchen

Chloe Wheatland is a content creator, model and plant-based recipe developer from Australia. She grew up in a cosy country town just north of Melbourne. She is a big believer in balance and living a lifestyle that fulfils her both physically and mentally. She became a vegan in her mid-teens due to her love and passion for animals, health and spirituality. Since that time her whole life has changed. Chloe discovered what she was truly passionate about and built a business from social media, where she is dedicated to sharing easy and healthy vegan recipes and mindfulness insights.

Chloe's Vegan Kitchen

90 fresh and easy recipes, from cookies to curries

CHLOE WHEATLAND

contents.

About	1
Food staples	4
Kitchen essentials	10

Breakfast

Good mornings create merry habits	15
Peanut butter and jam overnight oats	21
Avocado and garlic mushrooms on toast	22
Baked bananas with blueberry sauce	25
Spicy tofu scramble breakfast tacos	26
The best acai bowl	29
Bounty baked oats	30
Smoky baked beans	33
Matcha strawberry chia pudding	34
Pesto eggless frittatas	37
Snickez porridge	38
Cheesy breakfast polenta	41
Smoothies	42

Small plates and snacks

A small plate for six	49
Dips	52
Seeded crackers and cheese	59
Baked potato wedges with BBQ sauce	60
Grilled satay skewers	63
Chuna mousse crostini	64
Roasted carrots on whipped tofu	67

Salads and nourish bowls

You are perfectly imperfect	71
Roasted eggplant with creamy slaw bowl	77
Beetroot and cucumber bowl	78
Orange and sesame noodle salad	81
Falafel mezze bowl	82
Roasted cauliflower bowl	85
Mustardy potato salad	86
Polenta caprese salad	89
Butter bean Caesar	90
Black rice and rocket salad	93
Tex Mex salad	94
Broccolini and crispy tempeh salad	97

Budget recipes

Money is your buddy	101
Butternut pumpkin risoni	107
Sweet potato and rice tray bake	108
Mujadara inspired salad	111
Easy lentil bolognaise	112
Curried chickpea jacket potatoes	115
Simple tofu curry	116
Garlicky potato soup	119
Miso carrot pasta	120
Tray bake tacos	123
Couscous and sun-dried tomato salad	124
Sweet potato and capsicum soup	127
Roasted veg on whipped tahini	128

Quick dinners

Fear is wasting your time	133
Golden butter bean stew	139
The best (ever) vegan nachos	140
Creamy green pasta	143
Carrot noodle soup	144
Gochujang tofu burger	147
Eggy nasi goreng	148
Marry me gnocchi	151
Thai green curry	152
Rainbow peanut noodles	155
BBQ mushroom flatbreads	156
Cheat's dhal	159
Nut-free mac and cheese	160
Brothy coconut noodles	163
Cauliflower floret focaccia sandwich	164

No-bake desserts

Take the 'no-bake' path	169
No-bake carrot cake	173
Chickpea cookie dough	174
Protein balls	176
Chocolate cherry tart	181
Nutty caramel slice	182
Apple cream bark	185
Mini banoffee pies	186
Blueberry ice-cream bars	189
Mango matcha sorbet	190
Salted chocolate tahini fudge	193

Baked desserts

Get baked, not serious	197
Vanilla roasted plums with cinnamon cream	201
Spiced sweet potato and olive oil cake	202
Blueberry banana bread	205
Roasted dates with pistachio butter	206
Chunky chickpea cookies	209
Cheat's tiramisu	210
Strawberry shortcake trifles	213
Choc brownies with avocado frosting	214
Raspberry crumble	217
Easy cinnamon scrolls	218

Reference

Sample meal and mind plan	221
Conversion chart	226
Conclusion	227
Acknowledgements	229
Index	230

TAGS

I have included tags at the start of my recipes to give you some more information about the food before you start.

GF – gluten free
GFO – gluten free option
OF – oil free
RSF – refined sugar free

about.

Hey there,

My name is Chloe, and I am a vegan content creator, model and recipe developer from Australia. I come from humble beginnings, being raised by a strong and loving single mother in a small regional area called the Macedon Ranges. Roughly an hour out of Melbourne the area is known for its beautiful forests, artisan food, local wineries and, above all, Hanging Rock. Yes, the same Hanging Rock where those high-school girls mysteriously vanished on a picnic all those years ago. Or did they? Hate to break it to you, but the story is fake.

Ever since I was a child, I have been fascinated by health and food. I remember Friday being my favourite day of the week in primary school (aside from obvious reasons) because we had 'Fresh Fruit Fridays'. Every student got to choose a fresh piece of fruit to munch on during class. Why was this so exciting? Well, for one, we were never allowed to eat in class, so it made me feel like a total rebel. And two, I got to taste a different fruit each week. They even offered carrots on some weeks, which only made me feel even more rebellious in eating a VEGETABLE on fresh FRUIT Friday.

I continued to explore healthy food as I got older through cooking and eating, and I became aware of how food made me feel on both a physical and a mental level. I was also a total spirituality nerd, reading self-development book after self-development book until I began reciting their lines in my sleep. The first 'adult' book I read was *The Secret* by Rhonda Byrne when I was 10 years old, and let me tell you, I have never been more enthralled by a book in my life. Harry Potter had nothing on my self-development books (sorry J.K.).

Though I felt passionate about wellness as a child, I was constantly sick. Allergies, asthma, croup, bronchitis, seizures, bruises, gastro, you name it, I probably had it. By the time I went into high school, I was still struggling. I used to come home and need to nanny nap for a good hour on the couch before dance class. Considering I was only 14 years old, I remember thinking it was strange for my energy to be so low, but I shrugged it off and continued with the same lifestyle. It wasn't until two years later when a girl in my year level told me about how she had just converted to a vegan lifestyle that the shift began. I laughed veganism off initially. I could never do that. I needed protein, I needed nutrients and, most of all, I needed cheese. And lots of it. Later that week, a new documentary on Netflix appeared called *What the Health* and I kid you not, it was stalking me. I'd turn on the radio and they'd be speaking about it. I'd scroll on Instagram, and an ad for it would pop up. I even sat down in a café and the girls on the table next to me were talking about it. 'FINE, I'll watch it then,' I thought. Spoiler alert, it changed everything.

I was in shock about the impact that animal products have on our health and how animals are treated in agricultural farming. As a self-proclaimed animal lover, my stomach turned when I thought about all the animals I had consumed not only that day but during my whole existence. Trigger warning: skip this next sentence if you've got a queasy stomach. One scene that haunts me to this day is when they popped massive cysts on cows' butts then informed us there is a per cent allowance of how much pus commercially sold meat and dairy can contain. Are you kidding!? This whole time I've loved cheese but have unknowingly been eating cheese with a side of pus. That was it for me. Bye-bye animals, bye-bye pus and hello plants. That was at the end of 2017 and to this day, I'm still vegan. Just as I had hoped, my energy levels increased, my allergies and asthma ceased, my sleep improved and my skin, hair and nails were finally glowing! Thank you, plant lords.

A few months before going vegan, I had opened an Instagram account called '@sugarfreeteen'. Sarah Wilson's 'I Quit Sugar' franchise influenced mum and me to cut out refined sugars, so I began sharing sugar-free recipes. I had grown to what I thought at the time was a MAMMOTH following of 1000 people. As I got older and shifted to a vegan lifestyle, I continued to post. But due to the demands of school and my first years of work, I was lucky if I posted once a month. Flash forward to 2021. I was three years out of school, working as a social media manager for a local clothing store and doing part-time modelling, but something didn't feel right. I loved food, I loved health, and I desperately wanted to work for myself. I still had my Instagram account (which was now @chloeevegan) and considering I was coming from a social media background, taking Instagram more seriously seemed like the right direction.

So, I quit my job at the clothing store. The first few months were tough in every sense of the word: emotionally, financially and physically. I touch on this a lot in later chapters. Thankfully, however, it ended up being one of the best decisions of my life thus far. I was able to manifest the social media following and income I dreamed for myself. After a bunch of viral videos and a lot of hard work, my Instagram had grown from 5k followers to 265k within the space of a year and almost 1M within the space of two years, making it my full-time job. That's probably where you met me! So, hello again, I'm so grateful that you are here.

Let's get into the nitty-gritty of this book. If you've had a quick flick through, you'll notice that it's not just a regular cookbook. Yes, there are a bunch of delicious and easy plant-based recipes for you to cook and enjoy. But at the beginning of each recipe category, there is also a chapter dedicated to self-development and spirituality. Self-development has been a major part of my life for many years, and I attribute much of my success and continual growth to this area. I also truly believe that to be the best and healthiest versions of ourselves, our mindset, or in other words, how we think, feel, and believe about ourselves and the world around us, is just as important as what we eat and how often we exercise. By sharing my top mindfulness tips and tricks, as well as some of the most important life lessons I have learnt so far, I hope that this book gives you a more holistic approach to health than just the physical realm. I recommend reading the self-development chapter right before you make any of the recipes from that category so that you can nourish the mind and soul in preparation for nourishing the body.

So, without further ado, welcome to *Chloe's Vegan Kitchen*.

Chloe Wheatland

food staples.

Navigating the aisles of the supermarket or organic grocer, especially if you are new to experimenting with plant-based recipes, can feel daunting. My first trip to the supermarket as a vegan was quite the odyssey. I spent an hour squinting and straining my eyes to read the tiny ingredient labels on each product. Beware of the elusive 0.1% milk powder at the end of the list. The sneaky bugger almost got me every time. But now that I'm seven years into plant-based eating (and even longer by the time you read this book), supermarket shopping is a breeze. I'm in and out with five bags full in the same amount of time it used to take me to buy five individual items. So, I have compiled a list of my go-to ingredients that you'll always find sitting in my fridge or pantry, along with a sample grocery list that you can take with you to the supermarket. This section is purely for inspiration and by no means do you have to buy every single item on the list. Start slowly, experiment with different foods, and see what works for you, your lifestyle and your budget.

THE PANTRY

bananas: My favourite fruit. I love using them to sweeten baked goods or to freeze for banana nice-cream and smoothies. They are also a healthy source of carbohydrates, making them my favourite pre-workout snack. Pro tip: chopping your bananas before freezing them makes them easier to blend.

nut and seed butter: If you have followed me for a long time, you probably know that I am obsessed with peanut butter. Specifically, the smunchy kind. You know, half smooth and half crunchy. But other than that, nut and seed butters are a really great source of healthy fats and protein and are super versatile. You can add them to desserts or use them to create flavourful savoury sauces. I recommend opting for ones with just nuts and a touch of salt, avoiding added sweeteners, oils or fillers.

dried herbs and spices: Essential for bringing a bunch of flavour to your dishes! They have a long shelf life, and you only need small amounts for each dish, making them incredibly budget-friendly. My favourites are ground cinnamon, ground cumin, smoked paprika, ground turmeric, garlic powder, rosemary, thyme and chilli powder.

canned beans: A quick, easy and affordable source of protein to add to stir-fries, pasta dishes, curries and, in the case of chickpeas, even desserts!

rice and rice noodles: An easy-to-cook grain product that you can flavour and add to a range of dishes. There are also so many types of rice, all with different textures and flavours to explore. My favourites are basmati, brown and black rice.

oats: Oats are packed full of fibre and provide slow-burning energy to keep you energised throughout the day. They are also cheap, making them a great option for breakfast and as a base for desserts. Oats themselves are gluten-free, however the production lines they are made on in Australia are usually contaminated. That's why if you are gluten intolerant, I suggest purchasing gluten-free oats from online shops such as iHerb.

pasta: An easy and versatile way to bulk up dishes. You can make an endless number of different sauces to cover pasta in, add it to fresh salads or even bake it. For a higher protein or gluten-free option, I recommend opting for bean pasta. The taste and ease of cooking a good lentil pasta make it almost identical to the real thing.

sweet potato and potato: Potatoes are my definition of comfort food. They have a cosy and subtle taste, making them super easy to flavour for any dish. My favourite way to cook potatoes is by roasting them in the oven until crispy, but you can also boil, steam, fry or mash them to your preference.

dark chocolate: A good quality dark chocolate will take your desserts from good to great. I recommend opting for a refined sugar-free option that is at least 70% cocoa for extra richness, antioxidants, vitamins and minerals. But, if you don't love dark chocolate, there are also some great vegan milk chocolates out there that are also refined sugar-free. It might just mean ordering online as opposed to picking something off a supermarket shelf.

nutritional yeast: No, it's not like regular yeast. It's a type of deactivated yeast in the form of yellow flakes that adds a delicious savoury cheese flavour to dishes. It's also surprisingly high in B vitamins and protein.

nori or dulse flakes: An easy way to add iodine into your diet. I love sprinkling them on salads for a light and salty umami flavour.

olive oil: I'm not a fan of using heavy vegetable oils as they make me feel gross and oily (obviously). However, I don't mind using a bit of high-quality extra-virgin olive oil to crisp up ingredients or add to a fresh salad. It's high in monosaturated fats and has both anti-inflammatory and antioxidant qualities. The oil that I sometimes use for desserts is coconut oil. It's also a great way to smooth and thin out chocolate for melting.

tomato paste: An easy way to add a concentrated burst of tomato flavour to pasta dishes and curries. Pick one with minimal ingredients and at least 97% to 99% tomatoes.

rice malt syrup: My favourite liquid sweetener. It's fructose-free and has a thick, sticky consistency that is like honey. I love it for its subtle flavour that doesn't overpower a recipe as many other liquid sweeteners do. If you don't have rice malt syrup on hand, you can substitute it with any other liquid sweetener of your choice such as maple syrup or agave. However, as you'll see in my recipes, I do use rice malt syrup sparingly. I believe that you can almost get enough sweetness to your dishes just by adding fibre-packed fruits such as Medjool dates and bananas.

protein powder: Protein powder is not at all necessary to reach your protein intake on a plant-based diet. If you are consciously eating enough healthy legumes, grains, fruits, vegetables and nuts throughout the day, you can easily consume enough protein. However, I do think that it is an easy and convenient option for those who might not have as much time to focus on protein consumption. It's also a great way to add flavour to sweets and to thicken up batters for both baked and no-bake goods. I recommend organic protein powders with minimal and gut-friendly ingredients, avoiding sweeteners and numbers if possible. If you would prefer not to use protein powder, try substituting it with fine flour such as almond or oat flour, or reducing the amount of liquid in the recipe.

THE FRIDGE

plant-based milk: With so many plant-based milk options available, I encourage you to try out a few and pick a favourite. Opt for plant milks with minimal fillers, sweeteners and oils. You'll usually find these in the fridge section and not the long-life milk section. Personally, I love soy milk for its nutty flavour, creaminess and higher protein content. However, if you are new to plant milk and still adapting to the flavour, I always recommend starting with oat milk as I believe it has the most similar taste to dairy milk. For my recipes, feel free to substitute the plant milk I have suggested with your preference.

nuts and seeds: A must for adding creaminess, flavour and texture to sauces and no-bake desserts. They are also a great source of protein, healthy fats, and omega-3 and 6 fatty acids. I keep both my nuts and seeds in the fridge as it helps them to stay fresher for longer and, in the case of flax and chia seeds, avoids them going rancid. My fridge is always stocked with cashews, almonds, walnuts, pepitas, hemp seeds, sesame seeds, chia seeds and flaxseeds.

Medjool dates: Chewy, succulent and incredibly sweet, dates are by far my favourite way to sweeten desserts naturally. They are also packed with fibre and rich in magnesium, selenium and copper, making them a healthier alternative to other sweeteners. When processing dates, I always recommend soaking them in boiling water for 5 to 10 minutes first (or room temperature water overnight) to soften them and help your food processor out.

tofu: My most favourite vegan protein. It's made from soybeans and has a plain taste, making it super easy to flavour with different seasonings and sauces. As it has a high water content and spongy texture, I always suggest pressing your tofu for 5 to 20 minutes before cooking to remove excess liquid. It will give you creamier pieces that don't fall apart when cooking. To press tofu, you can use a tofu press or my go-to makeshift version which involves stacking a baking tray and putting one to two cookbooks on top. Only ever press firm tofu though, silken tofu will fall apart if pressed.

miso paste and tamari: Both made from fermented soybeans, these ingredients are easy and gut-friendly ways to add a salty umami flavour to savoury dishes.

avocado: Another obsession of mine. Avocado is creamy, smooth and so versatile. Smother it on toast, top it on tacos or even add it to chocolate desserts for added creaminess. It's also a great source of vitamin E and monosaturated fats.

fresh and frozen berries: I always have a good stock of fresh berries in my fridge to add to breakfast bowls or desserts. They add fresh pops of sweetness, colour, and a heap of vitamins and antioxidants. Frozen berries are great to have on hand for smoothies, freezer desserts and berry chia jams. They are also more budget-friendly and available all year round. My favourite berries are blueberries, raspberries and strawberries.

citrus: A healthy and vitamin C rich way to add acidity to both sweet and savoury dishes. My fridge is always stocked with fresh lemons and limes.

coconut yoghurt: A dairy-free alternative to yoghurt that I love. My favourite way to eat it is in breakfast bowls with granola and fresh berries or on top of warm desserts like cookies or berry crumbles. A dollop of plain coconut yoghurt is also delicious on curries or soups to soften the spice and add creaminess. I recommend buying unsweetened coconut yoghurt with added probiotics to support gut health.

sourdough bread: You can't go wrong with a thick and fluffy sourdough to dip into soups and sauces or smother in avocado. It is my favourite type of bread taste-wise and for gut health. For those with a gluten intolerance, I recommend opting for a grain or legume-based bread such as millet, linseed or red lentil. Just be sure to double-check the ingredient list as many gluten-free breads contain eggs.

GROCERY LIST

fruit and veg
- apples
- avocados
- bananas
- beetroot
- berries: blueberries, raspberries and/or strawberries
- broccolini and/or broccoli
- butternut pumpkin
- capsicum
- carrots
- cauliflower
- cucumbers
- garlic
- kale
- lemons and/or limes
- Medjool dates
- onions
- potatoes and/or sweet potatoes
- rocket
- spinach
- spring onions
- sun-dried tomatoes
- tomatoes
- zucchini

fresh herbs
- parsley
- coriander
- mint
- basil
- chives
- dill

nuts and seeds
- almonds and/or almond butter
- cashews
- chia seeds
- flaxseeds
- hazelnuts
- hemp seeds
- peanuts and/or peanut butter
- pine nuts
- tahini
- walnuts

legumes/proteins
- black beans
- butter beans
- cannellini beans
- chickpeas
- extra-firm tofu
- lentils
- silken tofu
- tempeh

grains
- oats
- soba noodles
- sourdough or seeded gluten-free bread
- pasta and/or bean pasta
- polenta
- quinoa
- rice and/or rice noodles

non-dairy subs
- soy, oat or your preferred plant milk
- coconut yoghurt
- vegan feta and/or parmesan

savoury cooking
- canned tomatoes
- red, green and/or yellow curry paste
- Dijon mustard
- chilli sauce
- miso paste
- nori sheets or dulse flakes
- nutritional yeast
- olive oil
- tamari
- tomato paste
- vegetable stock
- vegetable stock powder

dried herbs and spices
- black pepper
- Celtic sea salt
- chilli powder and/or flakes
- dried rosemary
- dried thyme
- ground cinnamon
- curry powder
- garlic powder
- ground coriander
- ground cumin
- ground turmeric
- onion powder
- smoked paprika

baking/sweets
- plain flour/plain gluten-free flour
- almond flour
- arrowroot flour
- baking powder
- cacao powder
- coconut oil
- chickpea flour
- dark chocolate
- desiccated coconut
- oat flour
- rice malt syrup
- vanilla extract
- vanilla protein powder

freezer
- frozen blueberries and/or raspberries
- frozen peas

drinks
- coconut water
- herbal tea
- ground coffee
- kombucha

kitchen essentials.

I never had access to a spiffy new food processor or high-quality knife set growing up. It wasn't until I left school and saved up by working as many casual jobs as I could fit within the space of 24 hours that I could afford to buy my own. I'm talking a 7:30 am wakeup to work at a café or clothing store (depending on which day it was) till 4 pm, then a restaurant from 5 pm to 10 pm before racing home to stuff my face with food and begin work on my laptop until 1 am creating social media content for local businesses. I had one day off, and that was Tuesdays. I often spent Tuesdays cooking different sweet and savoury recipes for mum and one of my best friends to try. At the time, banana nice-cream was trending on Instagram, and I desperately wanted to give it a go. So, out came my $40 blender and in went the frozen bananas. It took 30 minutes of blood, sweat and a whole lot of tears to blend those bananas. I had to add tablespoon after tablespoon of water just to get the damn blades to spin one rotation every minute. By the time the bananas were blended, I was left with a thin and watery banana smoothie. Which, don't get me wrong, was still edible. But it wasn't quite the thick banana nice-cream texture I was after. On that day, I decided to start saving up for my first Vitamix. When I had saved up enough to buy one, can you guess what was the first thing I made? Yep, banana nice-cream. And yep, my whole world changed.

You know the saying 'You get what you pay for'? Well, in terms of cookware and kitchen appliances, the saying is true. The more money you are willing or able to spend in the kitchen, the better-quality items you'll have and the quicker and easier your cooking experience will be. This is not to say that you can't cook with lower-priced versions of these utensils and appliances. Because you most certainly can. However, the process will be much more time-consuming. The texture of some recipes might also differ, as explained by the banana nice-cream incident. All I suggest doing is the best you can with the financial resources available to you and where possible, purchasing higher quality versions of the below items.

food processor and high-speed blender: A food processor is great for a lot of jobs but a high-speed blender is at the top of my list for a reason. It is, by far, the most used appliance in my kitchen. I use it for smoothie bowls, nut butter, soups, no-bake desserts, dips and more. The machine is also easy to use and compact, saving both time and space in the kitchen. I highly recommend purchasing a top-quality one, such as a Vitamix. I know they are on the dearer side, but as I mentioned earlier, I promise it will make cooking (and your life) so much easier. It's one of the best investments in the kitchen that I have ever made.

good quality knives: You know how chefs have this magical ability to chop ingredients almost too fast for your eyes to catch up with and still have every little piece looking perfectly shaped and sized? Unfortunately, I'm not one of those people. I chop like a regular human, at a regular speed with my sliced ingredients coming out looking, well, regular. But I can tell you that after spending too many years chopping ingredients with crappy knives from The Reject Shop, purchasing a good knife set is life changing. You don't realise how much more control a high-quality knife can give you over the ingredients you are chopping and how much prep time they can save. I recommend opting for weighty, sharp knives that fit well in your hands. Again, another investment, but a worthy one at that.

measuring cups and spoons: Unless a recipe relies on exact measurement to the gram (which mine don't), measuring cups and spoons allow you to follow a recipe quickly and easily. Good-quality ones are also relatively inexpensive and sold in most supermarkets. As I live in Australia, I use Australian metric measuring equipment. For my international friends, I have popped a conversion chart at the end of this book for you.

non-stick cookware: I only ever purchase non-stick, non-toxic pans and pots. They allow you to use less oil when cooking your favourite dishes and are a breeze to wash. Just avoid washing with metal scourers, as they damage the non-stick coating!

mixing bowls: I'm a sucker for a nice set of glass mixing bowls. They are easy to find, easy to wash and stack nicely in the cupboard. But what I love most about them is that you can see if there is anything clumped or stuck on the sides of the bowl that needs to be mixed in.

baking trays and silicon moulds: For oven-baked recipes, I recommend non-toxic stainless steel baking trays, muffin trays and loaf tins. However, for no-bake desserts that require the freezer, I recommend silicon moulds so that you can easily pop them out once set.

kettle: A common kitchen appliance, but one I wanted to include because of how often I use it. Nearly all my recipes that use cashews or dates require the kettle as they need to be soaked in boiling water to soften them before processing. Also, when I cook pasta or noodles, I pour hot water from the kettle into the pot so that the water begins to boil almost instantly once over heat on the stovetop.

breakfast.

good mornings create merry habits.

If you have ever seen *Hairspray* the movie, you'll know the iconic 'Good Morning Baltimore' scene. It's the very first scene and, in my opinion, the most exciting part of all. I swear I get a hit of dopamine every time I watch it. Tracy pops out of bed, sprays her big boofy hair and sings her way down the bustling streets of Baltimore. She dances past rats, waves at a 'flasher' and must catch a ride to school on a truck because she misses the bus. Yet, even after these typically 'negative' encounters, she is still smiling and singing about how 'Every day's like an open door'. Her zest for life gives her a positive perspective on everything and nothing seems to be able to knock her down. The question is, how can we bring this same zest for life and perspective into our daily lives? Obviously, we don't live in a musical and catching a ride on the top of a truck, whilst it looks fun, is both highly unlikely and incredibly risky. However, we do have the ability to cultivate this same magical feeling through our morning routine.

You've probably heard before that the morning is the most important time of the day. To that, I'd agree. It's the moment you open your eyes and decide what you want to think, do and, most importantly, feel throughout the day. If you're thinking 'Oi, Chloe. I don't wake up and decide to feel anxious, stressed, angry, fill in the blanks, throughout the day', then to that, I'd disagree. When you open your eyes, hit the snooze button three times, check your emails to find a new meeting scheduled at 2:30 pm when that's the time you had a dentist appointment booked (because, you know, your toothy hurty) and leave yourself 20 minutes to get ready for work, it's impossible to not feel overwhelmed. Your habitual morning actions are causing you to feel anxious, stressed, angry, fill in the blanks.

The law of attraction states that what we feel, we attract. Thus, the universe will only provide you with more reasons to feel anxious throughout the day. You get stuck in traffic on the way to work, your phone freezes in the middle of writing an urgent text and, just when you thought that it couldn't get any worse, someone in the office steals your lunch from the fridge. Let me tell you, the mix of feeling hungry and anxious is a whole new dimension of the emotional realm. Now, imagine that you woke up and decided to feel happy, excited, creative and inspired. What kind of actions do you think would help you to feel this way? I'm sure you have seen a billion people on Instagram flaunting their perfect morning routines. Waking up at 4 am, running a marathon, meditating on the beach, going for a morning swim, doing their skincare, and finishing with a green smoothie. I'm not going to lie, that morning routine does sound impressive, and I do love a good green smoothie. But, for me, a morning routine that extreme every day is unrealistic. I've tried to do something similar (minus the morning swim because I live closer to a forest than a beach). It lasted two days. I have also tried the 'opening your emails to a fistful of anxiety' morning routine too many times to count. What I can say about both is that neither worked and neither made me feel good. One made me feel insecure and time-poor and the other had me feeling like a ticking timebomb.

Your morning routine should not be overly complicated, exhausting or feel like a chore. Instead, it should fill you with so much love, energy and, as we saw with Tracy, zest for life, that when you rest your head on the pillow each night, you are so excited to wake up the next day and do it all over again. My go-to morning routine formula involves five simple tasks that can be personalised to suit you. You can also switch up the order of them as works best. I suggest waking up at least 30 to 40 minutes before you set your regular alarm (and going to bed 30 to 40 minutes earlier) to implement these practices into your day. Trust me, it is so worth it. I also suggest turning on the do not disturb or airplane mode on your phone when you go to sleep at night and leaving it on that mode until you have finished your morning routine. It just means that there will be zero notifications popping through to tempt you.

Now, let's get stuck into my go-to morning practices, **GMCMH**. Or, if you'd like a cute mnemonic, **G**ood **M**ornings **C**reate **M**erry **H**abits.

G – GRATITUDE

I don't currently have any tattoos and I'm undecided as to whether I will get any. But if I had to get a word tattooed on my body, it would be 'grateful'. It's just my favourite word. If you break it down into syllables, it's literally 'great' and then 'full'. That's just how I like to think of it every morning. What is **great** in my life that makes my heart **full**? It's an instant mood booster. The first thing I recommend doing in the morning is opening a journal, notepad or whatever you have that you can physically write on, and jotting down three things that you are grateful for. If this is your first time practising gratitude and you are finding it difficult to begin, here are a few prompts to get you started:

- I am grateful for my mum/dad/partner/sibling/friend because . . .
- I am grateful to live in . . . because . . .
- I am grateful to work as a . . . because . . .
- I am grateful to be able to . . . because . . .
- I am grateful to spend time doing . . . because . . .
- I am grateful to nourish my body with. . . because . . .

If you still can't think of any, let's go back to basics. If you are reading this right now, you most likely have eyes and the ability to see. Is that not something to be grateful for? Imagine all the smiles, sunsets or special moments you would have missed out on if it weren't for your sight. So, perhaps, your first gratitude entry could be something along the lines of 'I am grateful for the ability to see beautiful sunsets because they make me feel calm.' Practising gratitude forces you to stop, slow down and shift your perspective. You begin to look at the abundance in your life as opposed to the lack. You can feel a sense of pride about who you are, what you have and the world around you. Plus, if you are ever feeling down, because we can't always be as happy as Larry, you can flick open your journal and read through all the many reasons you have to smile. My gratitude entry this morning is: I am grateful that you are reading my book. Yay!

To follow this up, I also recommend writing down an affirmation or goal (or both) you want to achieve for the day. Both affirmations and goals work by repetition. The more you repeat them, the more you think about them and the more you attract situations in which you can achieve them. But to repeat them, we must remind ourselves of them a few times each day. You can do this by writing them on a sticky note and popping them somewhere you'll look at often. Your wallet, the fridge or, if you have a clear phone case like I do, in the back of your phone case is a great option. There are no rules to writing affirmations or goals, but there are definitely some pointers that I can give you. Let's start with the easier one, goals. Make sure the goal you choose to jot down is something small and achievable. If your goal is to become a millionaire tomorrow, then you'll probably feel deflated when you wake up with only a few dollars in your bank account and never want to write a goal again. But, if your goal is to cook one meal without using any animal products this week (hint, hint), then you are much more likely to achieve it and feel pride in yourself when you do. It's about being 1% better every day, not perfect.

Now to affirmations. These can be a bit more difficult because they require you to look at the things that don't make you feel so good and turn them into things that make you feel good. Another way of thinking about this is to see what areas of your life you feel could use improvement in and then speaking about them as if the improvement had already happened. Let me give you an example. When I first went full-time into social media and food content creation, I wasn't getting enough work. The lack of work was constantly on my mind and sending my stress levels through the roof. I remember checking my emails every five minutes like a maniac in the hope that a job would pop through. At the time I had very little savings and needed some dosh. So, I did what I knew best and turned to the power of affirmations. Here are three that I wrote, spoke and repeated every morning:

'People cannot wait to work with me.'
'People love watching me and are inspired by me.'
'I am exactly what people are looking for.'

Within three months of reciting these affirmations as if they were lyrics to my favourite song, and in conjunction with other mindset practices, I had more than enough work to keep me afloat. To this day, my growth in this area is continuing to expand. You can use affirmations for any area of your life that you want to grow in. Perhaps it's attracting a new relationship, car or holiday. Whatever it might be, write down what you want in a way that feels comfortable, exciting and attainable for you. Feel those words and repeat, repeat and repeat.

M – MEDITATION

The word meditation can sometimes scare people away. A bit like the word vegan can. Most people already have a perception of it, perhaps from previous experience or what they've heard from others, and so without actually taking the time to explore or practise it themselves, they reject it. The cool thing about meditation though is that it doesn't have to look the same for every person. It doesn't even have to look the same for you every day. Some mornings I wake up and I'm like yeah, I want to go full monk style, sit with my legs crossed and close my eyes in silence for 20 minutes. The next day, all I want to do is take a few deep breaths and imagine a white light travelling from the top of my head all the way down to my toes. When the mental chatter is at an all-time high, simply standing outside and observing the world around me without any thoughts or judgement does the trick. I suggest thinking of the word meditation as simply doing something to slow down your thoughts, listen to your breath and live in the present. I recommend dedicating between 5 to 20 minutes to this practice every morning for various reasons. For one, it's a quick way to feel more centred and relaxed. Two, there have been countless studies connecting it to improved sleep, mood, digestion, immune health and energy levels. And three, my most favourite reason of all, it inspires creativity and action. Nine out of 10 times my greatest ideas or revelations have come to me through a meditation when I was least expecting it. It's like one minute you are listening to the whistle of the wind in the distance and then boom, you create a budget recipe series on Instagram (if you are familiar with my two cheap series, that idea came from a meditation).

If you need help learning how to meditate, there are countless online resources that are free and easy to use. I recommend searching for guided meditations or frequency music on YouTube or Spotify or downloading the app Self-Timer and exploring that. Yes, that will require you to open a device. But if you keep do not disturb on, you should be able to avoid the distraction of notifications and quickly locate a good meditation.

C – CONCENTRATION

The broadest step of them all, but not one to be missed. Since we want our morning routine to help us to show up as our best selves for the remainder of the day, this step is what is going to boost our productivity and focus. It's about placing all your attention on *one* creative task for 5 to 10 minutes. This task could be:

- Reading a few pages of a book.
- Turning on an upbeat song and having a little boogie.
- Brainstorming a list of all the things you want to manifest.
- Sitting down and listening to your favourite podcast.
- Making your bed.
- Playing an instrument.
- Sketching something you love.
- Folding clothes, cleaning or ironing. Trust me on this one. There is something oddly satisfying about the repetitive action of housework.

Our brain works best when we are not multi-tasking (unfortunately). In fact, the brain can't multi-task, it can only switch back and forth between tasks. Training it every morning to dedicate its full attention towards one creative task at a time is not only a fun way to find inspiration through the task itself, but it's also a great way to strengthen your ability to focus. This will, in turn, help with your productivity levels throughout the day. Directing all your energy towards completing one task is a much more effective and time-efficient approach than having 50 tasks going on at once and needing to stop every five minutes to scroll on Instagram or check your emails because you forgot which task you were going to move on to.

M – MOVEMENT

When in the day do you most like to exercise? And how does that make you feel? I was always against morning workouts. I couldn't fathom the thought of waiting a whole extra 30 to 45 minutes before I could gobble up a delicious brekkie. It wasn't until I went solo travelling to Bali and attended a vegan fitness retreat that I was pushed to wake up at 4:30 am every morning and exercise. Not to mention, most of it was strength training. Considering I'm a HIIT and Pilates girlie, you can only begin to imagine how sore I was. When I got back home, I attempted to go back to my regular routine of exercising at 5 pm, just before dinner time. I had been struggling with some sleepless nights for a while before my Bali trip and after my first 5 pm workout back home, it happened again. I would also always have a random surge of energy and motivation at night, causing me to work on my phone or laptop late into the night and the early hours of the morning. Then it finally clicked. My 5 pm workout might be getting me physically ripped, but it was also ripping hours off my sleep schedule. This is not to say late workouts affect everyone this way, because they don't. I know plenty of people who go to the gym much later than 5 pm and still have a good night's sleep. For me, however, they were no longer working in alignment with my body. So, now I'm a morning workout type of person. They challenge, excite and energise me. I've noticed how much more productive I am during the day as opposed to solely at night. I also love that once it's over in the morning, I don't have to think about it for the rest of the day. More importantly, now when I tuck myself into bed, I fall asleep straight away and wake up feeling refreshed. Beauty sleep is a real thing! If working out in the morning is possible for you, I highly recommend giving it a try. Even if it's a quick 15-minute routine just to get you started. If working out in the morning doesn't suit you and you've tried many times, then I still recommend getting in movement in some form or another. Perhaps it's taking the dog for a walk, doing a 10-minute stretch or morning yoga flow, or even walking to work. Something that is going to get your blood pumping and release those feel-good endorphins.

H – HEALTH

Health, in this context, refers to a healthy breakfast. Something easy and delicious that is going to put you in a good mood and fuel you throughout the day. Luckily for you, you are currently reading a cookbook. And this cookbook just so happens to have an entire chapter dedicated to the best breakfasts out there. Whether you are a sweet or savoury morning person, or if you like to switch it up daily like me, pick the recipe you are craving and give it a go! For those pushed for time in the morning, I have also included some options that are great for meal prepping at the start of the week so that you can just open your fridge, grab and go.

peanut butter and jam overnight oats.

SERVES 4   **PREP TIME** 20 MINUTES   **SET TIME** 4 HOURS

These overnight oats are one of my favourite breakfasts to meal prep. They come together in 20 minutes and are ready for you to set and forget in the fridge. The best part is that you don't have to heat them the next morning. Just crack open the jar and dig in.

OVERNIGHT OATS
2 cups (180 g) rolled oats
1 cup (120 g) vanilla protein powder
2 tablespoons flaxseed meal
2¼ cups (565 ml) soy milk
¼ cup (70 g) peanut butter
2 tablespoons rice malt syrup
1 teaspoon vanilla extract

RASPBERRY CHIA JAM
2 cups (240 g) frozen raspberries, thawed
2 tablespoons chia seeds
1 teaspoon vanilla extract

TO SERVE (OPTIONAL)
fresh raspberries, peanut butter and soy milk

1. To prepare the overnight oats, place the rolled oats, protein powder and flaxseed meal into a large bowl. Mix well.
2. Add the soy milk, 1½ cups (375 ml) water, peanut butter, rice malt syrup and vanilla extract. Mix until well combined.
3. Divide the mixture equally among four jars and set aside in the fridge.
4. For the raspberry chia jam, combine the raspberries, chia seeds and vanilla extract in a large bowl and mash together with a fork. Allow to rest for 5 minutes or until the chia seeds have expanded and the mixture has become jam-like.
5. Spoon the raspberry chia jam on top of the overnight oats and set in the fridge for a minimum of 4 hours, or overnight.
6. When ready to eat, remove the overnight oats from the fridge. Add fresh raspberries, a dollop of peanut butter and a dash of soy milk to serve if you like.

TIP

These overnight oats can be kept in the fridge for 4–5 days. To switch up the flavour, you could substitute the raspberries with a different type of frozen berry or the peanut butter for cashew, almond or macadamia butter.

I show up as my best and most productive self every day.

breakfast.

avocado and garlic mushrooms on toast.

SERVES 3   **PREP TIME** 10 MINUTES   **COOK TIME** 20 MINUTES

The best savoury breakfast sides are avocado and garlic mushrooms. You can't tell me otherwise. They also both happen to be healthy, plant-based and quick to prepare. So, here is a breakfast showcasing the delicious duo.

GARLIC MUSHROOMS
2 punnets (400 g) button mushrooms, sliced
1 tablespoon tamari
1 tablespoon nutritional yeast
1 tablespoon olive oil
2 cloves garlic, finely diced
2 sprigs fresh thyme

TO SERVE
2 avocados, sliced
3 large slices sourdough bread (or your bread of choice)

TO SERVE (OPTIONAL)
vegan feta, olive oil and fresh thyme

1. To cook the garlic mushrooms, heat a frying pan over medium heat. Add the mushrooms and cook for 3–5 minutes without stirring. Flip and cook for another 5 minutes, without stirring, or until the liquid has reduced and mushrooms are beginning to brown.

2. Add the nutritional yeast and tamari and cook for a further minute, or until absorbed.

3. Add the olive oil, garlic and thyme and sauté for 3–4 minutes, stirring regularly, or until the mushrooms are golden and caramelised. Season well with salt and pepper and remove from heat.

4. Toast the bread slices and top with the sliced avocado. Spoon on the garlic mushrooms and add the vegan feta, olive oil and fresh thyme, if using.

TIP

For some protein, you can also top with ⅓ cup (55 g) of edamame beans.

I choose to release all that is not in alignment with me and embrace new beginnings.

baked bananas with blueberry sauce.

SERVES 2   **PREP TIME** 15 MINUTES   **COOK TIME** 10 MINUTES

This is a Sunday kind of breakfast. The kind of breakfast you don't want to spend too much effort making, but something more special than your everyday oats. The baked bananas go perfectly gooey and caramelised, the peanut protein whip adds creaminess, and the blueberry sauce brings a burst of sweetness.

BAKED BANANAS
1 tablespoon lemon juice
1 tablespoon rice malt syrup
½ teaspoon ground cinnamon
3 bananas, halved lengthwise

BLUEBERRY SAUCE
2 cups (280 g) frozen blueberries
1 tablespoon rice malt syrup
juice of ½ lemon
½ teaspoon vanilla extract
1 tablespoon arrowroot flour

PEANUT PROTEIN WHIP
1 cup (240 g) vanilla coconut
    yoghurt
⅓ cup (40 g) vanilla protein powder
2 tablespoons peanut butter

TO SERVE (OPTIONAL)
crushed peanuts

1. Preheat the oven to 220°C and line a baking tray with baking paper.

2. For the baked bananas, combine the lemon juice, rice malt syrup, cinnamon, and a pinch of salt in a small bowl. Place the bananas on the baking tray, cut side up, and brush over the cinnamon marinade. Bake for 10 minutes, or until softened and caramelised.

3. Meanwhile, to make the blueberry sauce, combine the frozen blueberries, rice malt syrup, lemon juice, vanilla extract and ¼ cup (60 ml) water in a saucepan. Whisk continuously over medium heat for 4 minutes or until the blueberries are soft and the mixture is bubbling.

4. Add the arrowroot flour and cook for a further minute or so, whisking continuously, until the mixture has thickened. Remove from the heat.

5. For the peanut protein whip, whisk the coconut yoghurt, vanilla protein powder and peanut butter in a large bowl until well combined, ensuring no lumps of protein powder remain.

6. To serve, dollop the peanut protein whip onto plates and spread with a spoon. Top with the baked bananas and spoon over blueberry sauce. Sprinkle with crushed peanuts, if using.

TIP

The baked bananas are best eaten the same day. Any leftover blueberry sauce and peanut protein whip can be stored in the fridge for up to 5 days.

Exciting opportunities present themselves to me all the time.

spicy tofu scramble breakfast tacos.

SERVES 3 **PREP TIME** 15 MINUTES **COOK TIME** 25 MINUTES

Every person has their favourite way to make a tofu scramble, so here's mine. It's easy, 'eggy' and has the perfect amount of spice. It's best eaten in these delicious breakfast tacos because, well, who wouldn't want to eat tacos for breakfast?

TOFU SCRAMBLE
1 cup (250 ml) oat milk
2 tablespoons nutritional yeast
1 tablespoon tahini
1 teaspoon chilli powder
½ teaspoon garlic powder
½ teaspoon smoked paprika
¼ teaspoon ground turmeric
1 tablespoon olive oil
1 shallot, finely chopped
375 g extra-firm tofu, pressed for 5 minutes and crumbled

SPICY CASHEW CREAM
½ cup (75 g) raw cashews
½ cup (125 ml) soy milk
1 clove garlic
1 tablespoon chilli sauce
1 tablespoon tomato paste
¼ teaspoon smoked paprika
juice of ½ lime

TO SERVE
6–9 corn tortillas
½ cup (80 g) cherry tomatoes, diced
400 g can black beans, drained and rinsed
1 avocado, mashed
¼ cup coriander, roughly chopped

1. To start the spicy cashew cream, soak the cashews in boiling water for 10 minutes, then drain.

2. Meanwhile, to make the tofu scramble, combine the oat milk, nutritional yeast, tahini, chilli powder, garlic powder, smoked paprika, turmeric and a pinch of salt and pepper in a small bowl. Whisk until well combined.

3. Heat the olive oil in a frying pan over medium heat. Add the shallot and sauté for 2–3 minutes, until translucent. Add the crumbled tofu and cook for 1–2 minutes, stirring occasionally, until beginning to brown.

4. Add the oat milk mixture and mix well to ensure all the tofu is coated. Cook for 4 minutes, stirring regularly, or until liquid has reduced. Remove from the heat, cover and keep warm.

5. To finish the spicy cashew cream, place the drained cashews, soy milk, garlic, chilli sauce, tomato paste, smoked paprika and lime juice into a food processor and add a pinch of salt and pepper. Process until smooth, stopping to scrape down the sides as needed. The sauce should be smooth and pourable. Add a dash more soy milk if needed.

6. Heat a frying pan over medium heat and toast the tortillas for 1–2 minutes on each side.

7. To assemble the tacos, dollop the spicy cashew cream onto tortillas and spread with a spoon. Top with the tofu scramble, cherry tomatoes, black beans, avocado and coriander.

TIP

To give the tofu scramble an even 'eggier' flavour, you can replace the pinch of salt with a pinch of black salt, also known as kala namak.

I nourish my body with healthy and delicious foods that energise me.

the best acai bowl.

SERVES 2–3   **PREP TIME** 15 MINUTES   **COOK TIME** 15 MINUTES

There is something about the combination of silky-smooth acai with the salty crunch of peanut butter that speaks to my soul. I eat at least three acai bowls per week, no matter the season, and have tried some from cafés all around Australia and even Bali. So, trust me when I tell you that I know what makes for a good one! Psst – there's even a sneaky serve of greens in mine.

OIL-FREE GRANOLA
1 cup (90 g) rolled oats
1 tablespoon hemp hearts
1 teaspoon ground cinnamon
2 tablespoons peanut butter
1 tablespoon rice malt syrup
1 tablespoon oat milk
1 teaspoon vanilla extract

ACAI BOWL
2 frozen bananas
2 × 200 g frozen acai packs
1 cup (140 g) frozen blueberries
½ cup (60 g) vanilla protein powder
1–2 handfuls baby spinach leaves
dash of soy or oat milk, if needed

TO SERVE (OPTIONAL)
peanut butter, fresh berries, sliced bananas and cacao nibs

1. Preheat the oven to 180°C and line a baking tray with baking paper.
2. To make the granola, mix the rolled oats, hemp hearts, cinnamon and a pinch of salt in a large bowl. Add the peanut butter, rice malt syrup, oat milk and vanilla extract and mix with your hands until the granola is clumpy.
3. Spread onto the baking tray and bake for 15 minutes, stirring halfway through, or until golden and crispy. Remove granola from the oven and allow to cool.
4. For the acai bowl, place the frozen bananas, acai, frozen blueberries, vanilla protein powder and spinach into a high-speed blender. Blend until thick and smooth, stopping to scrape down the sides as needed. Add a dash of soy or oat milk if needed to help the mixture move in the blender.
5. Scoop the acai into serving bowls and top with the granola. Add a dollop of peanut butter, fresh berries, sliced banana and cacao nibs, if you like.

TIP

This is a recipe that I highly, HIGHLY, recommend investing in a high-quality blender for. I love the Vitamix because it comes with a tamper that allows you to press the frozen bananas towards the blades for a quicker and smoother blend.

I am allowed to take time out for myself in the morning.

bounty baked oats.

SERVES 8   **PREP TIME** 15 MINUTES   **COOK TIME** 30 MINUTES

Baked oats are another one of my go-to meal prep breakfasts. You can make a batch of them at the start of the week, divide them up and have them wrapped and ready to go in the fridge for your mornings. These oats are my favourite because they taste like you are eating chocolate coconut cake for breakfast, only they are healthier, plant-based and have a good serving of protein.

BAKED OATS
1 cup (150 g) Medjool dates, pitted
3 cups (750 ml) soy milk, plus more if needed
½ cup (130 g) almond butter
1 teaspoon vanilla extract
2 cups (180 g) rolled oats
1 cup (80 g) desiccated coconut
½ cup (60 g) vanilla protein powder
⅓ cup (35 g) cacao powder
½ cup (95 g) dark chocolate chips

VANILLA PROTEIN WHIP
2 cups (480 g) vanilla coconut yoghurt
⅓ cup (40 g) vanilla protein powder
½ teaspoon vanilla extract

TO SERVE (OPTIONAL)
cacao powder

1. Preheat the oven to 175°C and lightly grease a 2L glass baking dish (28 cm × 20 cm).

2. To make the baked oats, soak the dates in boiling water for 5 minutes, then drain. Place the dates into a large bowl and mash until sticky and clumpy. Add the soy milk, almond butter and vanilla extract and mix well.

3. Add the rolled oats, desiccated coconut, protein powder, cacao powder and a pinch of salt. Mix until smooth and well combined. The mixture should be thick, creamy and scoopable. Add more soy milk if too thick and more oats if too thin.

4. Fold the chocolate chips through and pour the mixture into the baking dish. Bake for 25–30 minutes, or until the top has deepened in colour and a skewer comes out clean. Allow to cool for 10 minutes.

5. Meanwhile, for the vanilla protein whip, combine the coconut yoghurt, vanilla protein powder and vanilla extract in a large bowl. Whisk until well combined, ensuring no lumps of protein powder remain.

6. To serve, slice the baked oats into 8 equal pieces. Transfer to a serving plate and top with the vanilla protein whip. Dust some cacao powder over the top, if you like.

TIP

If making for meal prep, I recommend heating up a portion in the morning in the microwave for 30 seconds or popping it in a preheated 180°C oven for 5 minutes.

I am able to focus my attention on one task at a time.

smoky baked beans.

SERVES 3   **PREP TIME** 10 MINUTES   **COOK TIME** 20 MINUTES

I loved canned baked beans as a kid. So much so that I would be happy to eat them cold and straight from the can. Gross, I know. These, however, take the crown for the best baked beans out there. They are rich, tomatoey and full of smoky flavour. Of course, they do take a bit more time and effort than opening a can. I promise that it is worth it, both taste- and health-wise.

BAKED BEANS
1 tablespoon olive oil
½ brown onion, diced
1 clove garlic, finely chopped
1 teaspoon smoked paprika
½ teaspoon dried thyme
2 tablespoons tomato paste
1 tablespoon rice malt syrup
1 tablespoon tamari
1 tablespoon balsamic vinegar
2 teaspoons Dijon mustard
2 × 400 g cans cannellini beans, drained and rinsed
400 g can diced tomatoes
½ cup (125 ml) vegetable stock

TO SERVE
4 large slices sourdough bread (or your bread of choice)

TO SERVE (OPTIONAL)
simple cashew cream (page 57), chopped flat-leaf parsley and chilli flakes

1. Heat the olive oil in a saucepan over medium heat. Add the onion and sauté for 2–3 minutes, until translucent. Add the garlic, smoked paprika and thyme and sauté for a further 30 seconds or until fragrant.
2. Add the tomato paste, rice malt syrup, tamari, balsamic vinegar and Dijon mustard and mix well. Cook for 2 minutes, stirring regularly, or until browned and bubbling.
3. Stir in the cannellini beans, diced tomatoes, vegetable stock and a pinch of salt and pepper. Reduce heat to low. Simmer, covered, for 10 minutes, stirring occasionally. Uncover and cook for a further 3–5 minutes, stirring regularly, until thickened. Remove from heat.
4. Meanwhile, toast the bread slices.
5. Spoon the baked beans into bowls and serve with the toast. If you like, add a dollop of cashew cream and a sprinkle of parsley and chilli flakes.

TIP

These beans are also delicious in a breakfast wrap, bowl or tacos!

I wake up with excitement for the day.

breakfast.

matcha strawberry chia pudding.

SERVES 4   PREP TIME 15 MINUTES   SET TIME 2 HOURS

Can breakfast on the go get any more gorgeous? This is my thick and creamy matcha chia pudding with strawberry jam and a big dollop of coconut yoghurt. It's packed with fibre and omega-3 fatty acids and takes under 15 minutes to make.

MATCHA CHIA PUDDING
1½ cups (375 ml) soy milk
½ cup (120 g) coconut yoghurt
2 tablespoons rice malt syrup
1½ teaspoons matcha powder
1 teaspoon vanilla extract
½ cup (100 g) chia seeds

RAW STRAWBERRY JAM
350 g fresh strawberries, stems removed
1 tablespoon chia seeds
½ teaspoon vanilla extract

TO SERVE (OPTIONAL)
coconut yoghurt, sliced strawberries and matcha powder

1. For the matcha chia pudding, combine the soy milk, coconut yoghurt, rice malt syrup, matcha powder and vanilla in a large bowl. Whisk vigorously until smooth, ensuring no lumps of matcha remain. Add the chia seeds and mix until well combined. Allow to sit for 10 minutes.

2. Meanwhile, for the raw strawberry jam, place the strawberries into another bowl and mash with your hands until juicy but with some strawberry chunks remaining. Mix in the chia seeds and vanilla extract. Allow to sit for 5 minutes so that the chia seeds absorb the strawberry juice and expand.

3. Give the matcha chia pudding a good stir and equally divide among four jars. Top each with the strawberry jam and set in the fridge for 2 hours, or overnight.

4. When ready to eat, remove from the fridge and add a dollop of coconut yoghurt, some sliced strawberries and a dusting of matcha powder, if you like.

TIP

Store these in the refrigerator for up to 4 days.

I set positive intentions for the day ahead, knowing that I attract what I focus on.

pesto eggless frittatas.

SERVES 3   **PREP TIME** 20 MINUTES   **COOK TIME** 40 MINUTES

These are for my savoury breakfast lovers who still want to meal prep but aren't keen on oats. They are protein-rich, easy to make and pack so much flavour from the bright and punchy basil pesto.

350 g extra-firm tofu, pressed for 5 minutes and drained
¾ cup (180 ml) soy milk
¼ cup (15 g) nutritional yeast
2 tablespoons arrowroot flour
2 tablespoons tahini
1 teaspoon garlic powder
½ teaspoon vegetable stock powder
¼ teaspoon ground turmeric
3 tablespoons chunky pesto (page 55)

TO SERVE (OPTIONAL)
simple cashew cream (page 57) and chilli oil

1. Preheat the oven to 180°C and grease a 6-hole 7.5 cm × 4.5cm silicon muffin tray.
2. Place the tofu, soy milk, nutritional yeast, arrowroot flour, tahini, garlic powder, vegetable stock powder, turmeric and a pinch of salt and pepper into a food processor. Process until smooth.
3. Spoon the mixture into the muffin tray, dividing evenly between the holes. Top each frittata with ½ tablespoon of pesto and swirl in with a skewer to create a marbled effect.
4. Bake for 35 minutes, or until set and the tops are golden. Remove from the oven and allow to cool for 10 minutes.
5. Pop frittatas out of the muffin tray. Serve with a dollop of cashew cream and a drizzle of chilli oil, if using.

TIP

These are also a great school snack for the kiddos! They'll fit right into the lunchbox and are just as delicious when eaten cold.

I am filled with love and gratitude for another day on Earth.

snickez porridge.

SERVES 3   **PREP TIME** 5 MINUTES   **COOK TIME** 5 MINUTES

You'd think that porridge is the very last thing you'd want on the hot, humid and sweaty island of Bali. Well, at least that's what I thought until a friend convinced me to try the 'snickez porridge' from a café in Canggu. It was creamy, chocolatey and by far the best porridge I have ever eaten. So much so that it serves as the inspiration for this recipe!

1 banana, mashed
2 cups (500 ml) soy milk, plus ¼ cup (60 ml), to serve
2 tablespoons peanut butter
1 teaspoon vanilla extract
1 cup (90 g) rolled oats
2 tablespoons cacao powder

TO SERVE (OPTIONAL)
peanut butter, dark chocolate squares and toasted desiccated coconut

1. Combine the banana, soy milk, peanut butter and vanilla extract in a saucepan and mix well.
2. Add the rolled oats, cacao powder and a pinch of salt. Whisk until well combined, ensuring no clumps of cacao powder remain.
3. Place the saucepan over high heat. Once bubbling around the edges, reduce heat to low. Cook for 5 minutes, stirring regularly, or until thickened.
4. Remove from the heat and divide among serving bowls. Pour over extra soy milk and top with a dollop of peanut butter, dark chocolate squares and toasted desiccated coconut, if you like.

TIP

If you love adding protein powder to your oats, feel free to add a scoop of vanilla protein powder with an extra ¼ cup (60 ml) soy milk.

I am the creator of my best reality.

cheesy breakfast polenta.

 GF RSF

SERVES 3–4   **PREP TIME** 15 MINUTES   **COOK TIME** 25 MINUTES

Polenta is made of ground corn and is gluten-free. It has a lush and creamy texture and is one of my favourite budget-friendly ways to bulk up meals. I've paired it here with roasted tomatoes, spinach and chimichurri for a filling and flavourful breakfast bonanza.

ROASTED VINE TOMATOES
30 cherry tomatoes, on the vine
2 teaspoons olive oil
1 teaspoon dried thyme

CHIMICHURRI
½ cup flat-leaf parsley, chopped
¼ cup oregano leaves, chopped
1 clove garlic, finely chopped
1 red chilli, seeds removed and finely chopped
juice of ½ lime
¼ cup (60 ml) olive oil

WILTED SPINACH
1 tablespoon olive oil
1 small clove garlic, finely chopped
300 g baby spinach

POLENTA
2 cups (500 ml) vegetable stock or water
2 cups (500 ml) soy milk
1 cup (170 g) instant polenta
¼ cup (15 g) nutritional yeast
1 tablespoon olive oil

TO SERVE (OPTIONAL)
vegan feta and chopped flat-leaf parsley

1. Preheat the oven to 220°C and line a baking tray with baking paper.
2. To cook the roasted vine tomatoes, place the tomatoes on the baking tray. Drizzle with the olive oil, sprinkle with thyme and season with a pinch of salt and pepper. Rub with your hands to coat each tomato. Roast for 25 minutes, or until the tomato skins have softened and split.
3. Meanwhile, for the chimichurri, mix all the ingredients in a small bowl until well combined. Transfer to a jar and set aside.
4. To prepare the wilted spinach, heat the olive oil in a large frying pan over medium heat. Add the garlic and sauté for 1 minute. Add the spinach and cook, tossing and stirring occasionally for 1–2 minutes, until wilted. Season with a pinch of salt and pepper and remove from heat. Cover and keep warm.
5. For the polenta, place the stock or water, soy milk and a pinch of salt and pepper into a saucepan. Mix well and bring to the boil over high heat. Reduce heat to medium and slowly pour in the polenta and nutritional yeast, whisking constantly. Cook for about 2 minutes, still whisking, until thickened. Remove from heat and whisk in the olive oil.
6. To serve, dollop the polenta onto serving plates and spread with a spoon before it cools. Top with the roasted vine tomatoes, wilted spinach and a drizzle of chimichurri. If you like, add some vegan feta and parsley.

TIP

Polenta is best eaten as soon as it is ready, as it firms up as it cools. To reheat any leftovers, break up the polenta in a saucepan and add a dash of water or soy milk. Heat over low heat, whisking to remove any lumps, until smooth and hot.

I move my body in the morning with ease and comfort.

smoothies.

You can never go wrong with a good smoothie. And by good smoothie, I mean one that tastes delicious and keeps you feeling full. By adding a healthy fat, protein source and carbohydrate to each of these smoothies, you won't get that grumbling feeling in your stomach 10 minutes after you've taken your last slurp. These smoothies are also great to share as a side to a savoury breakfast with a loved one or as a post-workout snack with your workout buddy.

strawberries and cream.

GF OF RSF

SERVES 1–2   **PREP TIME** 5 MINUTES

1 cup (150 g) frozen strawberries
½ cup (60 g) frozen raspberries
1 frozen banana
⅓ cup (40 g) vanilla protein powder
⅓ cup (85 g) vanilla coconut yoghurt
2 tablespoons hemp seeds
1 cup (250 ml) soy or oat milk, plus extra if needed

TO SERVE (OPTIONAL)
coconut yoghurt and halved strawberries

1. Combine all the ingredients in a blender. Blend until smooth, adding more soy milk if you want to make it slightly less thick.

2. If you like, brush coconut yoghurt on the insides of a tall glass (or 2 smaller glasses) before pouring in the smoothie. Garnish with strawberries, if using.

TIP

For the plant milk in each smoothie, I have listed soy or oat as they are the two I use most frequently. Keep in mind that if protein is a macronutrient you want to increase, soy milk will bump up the protein content of each. However, you are not limited to these two options. Almond milk and coconut water are also great substitutes.

mocha hazelnut.

GF OF RSF

SERVES 1–2   **PREP TIME** 5 MINUTES

2 Medjool dates, pitted
1 frozen banana
150 g silken tofu
1½ tablespoons cacao powder
1 tablespoon freeze-dried instant coffee
1 tablespoon hazelnut butter
½ cup (125 ml) soy or oat milk,
  plus extra if needed

TO SERVE (OPTIONAL)
melted dark chocolate, roughly chopped hazelnuts

1. Soak the dates in boiling water for 5 minutes, then drain.

2. Combine the remaining ingredients, dates and a pinch of salt in a blender. Blend until smooth, adding more soy milk if you want to make it slightly less thick.

3. For a fun serving option, drizzle melted dark chocolate around the inside of a tall glass (or 2 smaller glasses) before pouring in the smoothie. Top with chopped hazelnuts, if using.

Today I choose to align myself with growth and joy.

breakfast.

miso date caramel.

SERVES 1–2 **PREP TIME** 5 MINUTES

2 Medjool dates, pitted
1 frozen banana
⅓ cup (40 g) vanilla protein powder
2 tablespoons cashew or macadamia butter
2 teaspoons white miso paste
1 teaspoon maca powder
1 cup (250 ml) soy or oat milk,
 plus extra if needed

TO SERVE (OPTIONAL)
cashew butter and ground cinnamon

1. Soak the dates in boiling water for 5 minutes, then drain.
2. Combine the remaining ingredients, dates and a pinch of salt in a blender. Blend until smooth, adding more soy milk if you want to make it slightly less thick.
3. If you like, brush cashew or macadamia butter on the inside of a tall glass (or 2 smaller glasses) before pouring in the smoothie. Sprinkle with cinnamon, if using.

creamy mango and pineapple.

SERVES 1–2 **PREP TIME** 5 MINUTES

1 cup (150 g) frozen chopped mango
½ cup (75 g) frozen chopped pineapple
pulp of 1 passionfruit
⅓ cup (40 g) vanilla protein powder
¼ cup (60 g) vanilla coconut yoghurt
1¾ cup (430 ml) soy or oat milk,
 plus extra if needed

TO SERVE (OPTIONAL)
coconut yoghurt and hemp hearts

1. Combine all the ingredients in a blender. Blend until smooth, adding more soy milk if you want to make it slightly less thick.
2. Pour the smoothie into a tall glass (or 2 smaller glasses). Top with coconut yoghurt and hemp hearts if you like.

mint choc chip.

SERVES 1–2 **PREP TIME** 5 MINUTES

2 frozen bananas
½ ripe avocado
1 handful baby spinach leaves
¼ cup mint leaves
150 g silken tofu
½ teaspoon vanilla extract
1 ¼ cups (310 ml) soy or oat milk
2 tablespoons cacao nibs

TO SERVE (OPTIONAL)
cacao nibs and mint leaves

1. Place all the ingredients except the cacao nibs into a blender. Blend until smooth, adding more soy milk if you want to make it slightly less thick. Add the cacao nibs and pulse on and off for 20 seconds.

2. Pour the smoothie into a tall glass (or 2 smaller glasses). Garnish with more cacao nibs and mint leaves, if you like.

Every new day is an opportunity for me to achieve my goals.

breakfast.

small plates and snacks.

a small plate for six.

When I was 13 years old, I had a fallout with one of my best friends. In hindsight, it was a blessing in disguise. At the time, however, it was rough. Especially when you're in high school and every Jack and Jill feels the need to gossip about it and take a side. I wasn't one of the 'cool' kids, so I drew the short straw. It was my first year of high school and the majority of my year level already had a vendetta against me over a silly friendship debacle. One day I came home sobbing after hearing some nasty comments circulating about me. I confided the whole ordeal to a family friend who was visiting. What he said next changed my perspective on relationships forever. He grabbed my left hand and opened my palm. He said that this was the hand of lessons. It's for the people who come and go from our lives but teach us something along the way. He then grabbed my right hand and counted down each finger. He said this is the hand of choice. It's for the people you choose to have in your inner circle. He then asked me which hand my former friend belonged in. Those words still resonate with me today. People come and go from our lives and that is okay. They appear when the time is right to impart a lesson. Whether you define that lesson as good or bad is inconsequential. It is just something the universe believes we need to experience and grow from. When we have learned all we are meant to from that person, our paths will naturally diverge, making space for new connections. Our left hand, in this sense, is infinite. We will have a constant rotation of people coming and going from our lives. Our right hand is more stable because it's up to us to decide who belongs there. It is the five people we choose to hang out with the most. As we get to select these people, they should be those who support, empower, push and inspire us. There is no rule saying that you are limited to five people. However, the smaller the crew, the better. The more time we can dedicate to those who help us to thrive (the right-hand crew), the easier it will be to manage and set boundaries within other relationships (the left-hand crew).

I'm sure you've heard somewhere before that we become who we surround ourselves with. Ever noticed how you and your best friend both say the same words, laugh at the same jokes and accidentally rock up wearing the same outfit without planning it? And, in the case of girls, you might even have your period at the same time. There actually is a scientific explanation for this based on pheromones, but that's a topic for a different book. What I'm trying to say is the more time you spend with someone, the more you become like them. If you don't like the way the people closest to you treat you, other people, or themselves, then it's time to re-evaluate your relationship with them because soon you aren't going to like the person you've become. I'm not suggesting saying 'See ya b*tch' and ghosting them like you did your last Tinder date. I'm simply suggesting setting boundaries. Moving them from your right hand to your left hand so you can free up the space for a new rightie to settle in. An easy way to see whether the people closest to you deserve a spot in your right hand is to ask yourself, how do you feel when you're around them? If you're a visual learner like me, writing it down with pen and paper might be a good place to start. I suggest exploring the answers to the following questions:

1. What do you have in common? Is it surface-level stuff? Such as living in the same area or having parents that are friends. Or is it stuff on a deeper, more emotional, and intellectual level? For example, do you share similar views on spirituality? Do you both love health and fitness? Do you both have careers that you are passionate about?

2. What do you talk about with them? Are you sharing your goals and aspirations for the future or are you gossiping about another friend because you don't like their new hairstyle?

3. How do they make you feel? You deserve to have people in your life who support and encourage you. You deserve to have people that celebrate your wins and want to see you thrive. You deserve to experience love in every relationship. If you have people that make you feel anything less than that, then they aren't the right people for you. Side note, no one can 'make' you feel a certain way. The question is more, how do you choose to feel around them based on your conversations?

4. Are they an energiser or an energy stealer? Do you leave the conversation feeling inspired or do you feel as if you need a nap to recover? I have been friends with some energy stealers in my life and have come home to have an hour-long nap after seeing them. And this is coming from someone who NEVER day naps.

5. The last and most important question is, do they deserve a place in your right hand? This one is simple. It's a yes or a no.

If you've decided that someone in your inner circle is no longer serving the person you are or want to become, I suggest implementing boundaries between you two. It does not mean ruling them out of your life completely, just introducing some ways that can foster a healthier relationship between you both. I have a friend that I have known since I was a child. I love and adore her so much that I want to squeeze her every time I see her. She is one of the funniest people I've met and the time we share we spend laughing for the majority of it. However, we are different creatures when it comes to nightlife. I'm a homebody. I get pleasure out of entertaining and cooking for people at home. Occasionally, I love visiting a nice restaurant and a cosy bar for a few wines after. My friend, on the other hand, is a party girl. She's still up dancing by the time my morning alarm goes off. After a few trials and tribulations in our relationship, we decided that it was best for us to catch up as much as we can during the day as opposed to solely the night. So, by the end of the night, we aren't feeling flat and deflated when we realise our values in that area don't align. That is our friendship boundary, and we implement it as much as possible.

If you feel you are in relationships that don't serve you at all, that's ok too. My biggest advice would be to let them go. If this is scary, I understand. I've had times in my life when I've held onto friendships and even romantic relationships out of a fear of loneliness as opposed to getting any value out of them. What I've learnt is that when you release those people, you open the space for new people to come into your life. However, to move on from a relationship, you must have an open conversation with the person about it. No one likes being left in the dark. It's cruel and confusing. Shedding light on why you feel that neither of you is a good influence on each other will give you both the clarity needed to move forward. The conversation might also give them food for thought to reflect on the person they've become, initiating positive change in their life. Of course, it's not always going to be that easy. Be cautious where you decide to have the conversation. The person might cause a kerfuffle in the middle of a café and scream 'a**hole' at you whilst they storm out the door. But life keeps on going. They'll get over it, you'll get over it, and more importantly, you'll have opened the space to meet new people who are in alignment with you. Just don't forget to leave the poor barista a tip as you leave the café.

I understand that making friends as an adult is harder than when we were younger. School, sports and clubs forced us to be in small spaces with others for years. We were bound to click with at least one person or another. The real world, however, is much different. Especially in this day and age when so many of us have the opportunity to work from home as opposed to the confines of an office. The beginning of my social media career felt lonely. I was by myself for much of the day, cooking, filming and editing. It wasn't until I started actively looking for friends who shared the same values and interests as me that some beautiful people came into my life. I signed up for gym classes, travelled domestically and internationally, and attended countless events in the food and fashion space. One of the most rewarding and exciting ways I connected with like-minded people was by signing up for a vegan fitness retreat in Bali where everyone shared the common interests of health, fitness, animals and the planet. It's all well and good to acknowledge that you want new friends, but nothing about it is going to happen unless you take the next step. If you love art, sign up for an art class. If you love reading, sign up for a book club. If you love running, sign up for a run club. Apparently, they are also the new Tinder, so you might find a love interest there as well. Double win! Whatever you can do to get yourself out there and mingling with people who share the same interests as you, do it.

We should also aspire to be friends with people who inspire us; people who are growing in the direction you want to grow in. For me, I wanted to be friends with people making waves in my industry. I followed other creators online who inspired me and messaged them. Just a quick hello and thank you for their content. Some responded, others didn't. But many of the ones who got back to me were kind enough to share tips on how to excel in the online space. Just from those initial messages, I've developed some incredible friendships with other creators. I feel so fortunate to be able to trade tips and tricks with them as well as celebrate our viral videos and exciting opportunities. The cool thing about being friends with those who inspire you is that they also challenge you. My social media feed is filled with posts so creative and unique from other creators that it pushes me to want to go to those lengths with my content. If you were to look at my content and recipes from two years ago compared to today, the difference is painstakingly obvious. I dedicate a lot of that to studying other creators and wanting to refine my craft to their level.

If you take anything from this chapter, let it be this: be selective in whom you choose to surround yourself with. The biggest way humans learn and grow is through other people. Thus, those you spend the most time with will influence how you think, feel, perceive, decide and act every single day. You become a direct reflection of your right-hand crew. If you don't feel inspired, loved, or energised by those people, knock them to your left hand by setting boundaries. Or, if need be, let go of them completely. It is ok to do so. Trust your gut. You will know what the right call is. In this recipe chapter, I have created a bunch of small plate and snack recipes. Can you guess how many each recipe serves? Yup, six people. A serve for you and a serve for each member of your right-hand crew for picnics, barbecues or dinner parties. You are worthy of incredible relationships, and to share these delicious small plates and snacks with them.

dips.

I like to think of dips as the jewellery to a good meal, enhancing the allure with their creamy textures and punchy flavours. They add an extra piece of pizzaz. However, their charm extends beyond complementing meals; they shine just as brightly when enjoyed as standalone snacks or as part of a platter accompanied by crackers, veggie sticks and fluffy slices of Turkish bread. So, let's celebrate a girl's best friend, not diamonds, but dips.

TIP

Each dip is best kept for up to 4 days in an airtight container in the fridge. For extra freshness and to avoid drying out, drizzle a light layer of olive oil on top before storing.

small plates and snacks.

pink beetroot hummus.

GF RSF

SERVES 6   **PREP TIME** 10 MINUTES

400 g can chickpeas, drained and rinsed
1 clove garlic
juice of ½ lemon
¼ cup (70 g) tahini
2 cooked baby beetroot
   (from vacuum sealed pack)
3 ice cubes

TO SERVE (OPTIONAL)
olive oil, sesame seeds and vegan feta

1. Place the chickpeas, garlic, lemon juice, tahini, baby beetroots, ice cubes and a pinch of salt and pepper into a food processor.

2. With the motor running, slowly add 1 tablespoon of water. Process for about 2–3 minutes, stopping to scrape down the sides as needed, until smooth. Add a little more water if you think it is too thick.

3. Transfer the beetroot hummus to a serving bowl. If you like, drizzle with olive oil and sprinkle with sesame seeds and vegan feta.

roasted garlic hummus.

SERVES 6   PREP TIME 10 MINUTES
COOK TIME 45 MINUTES

1 head garlic, skin left on
2 teaspoons olive oil
400 g can chickpeas, drained and rinsed
juice of ½ lemon
¼ cup (70 g) tahini
¼ teaspoon ground cumin
3 ice cubes

TO SERVE (OPTIONAL)
olive oil, pepper and roasted garlic clove

1. Preheat the oven to 200°C.
2. Cut about 1 cm off the top of the head of garlic. It should be enough to expose the top of the garlic cloves. Place onto a sheet of foil, cut side up, and drizzle with the olive oil. Wrap the garlic in the foil and place it on a baking tray.
3. Roast for 40–45 minutes, until the cloves are golden and tender. Remove from the oven and allow to cool.
4. Squeeze the roasted garlic out of the garlic skin, into a food processor. Add the chickpeas, lemon juice, tahini, ground cumin, ice cubes and a pinch of salt and pepper. With the motor running, slowly add 2 tablespoons of water. Process for about 2–3 minutes, stopping to scrape down the sides as needed, until smooth.
5. Transfer the hummus to a serving bowl. If you like, drizzle with olive oil, pepper and an extra clove of roasted garlic.

There are people out there who value my perspective.

small plates and snacks.

spicy capsicum and walnut dip.

SERVES 6   **PREP TIME** 10 MINUTES
COOK TIME 45 MINUTES

3 red capsicums, cut into quarters, seeds removed
1 tablespoon olive oil
1 cup (100 g) walnuts
2 cloves garlic
juice of ½ lemon
1 teaspoon ground cumin
½ teaspoon smoked paprika
½–1 teaspoon chilli powder

TO SERVE (OPTIONAL)
olive oil and chopped walnuts

1. Preheat oven to 200°C and line a small baking tray with baking paper.

2. Place capsicum on the baking tray. Drizzle with the olive oil and rub with your hands to coat evenly. Roast for 30–35 minutes, until the capsicum is tender and charred.

3. Remove the capsicum from the oven, place into a large bowl and cover with plastic wrap. Allow to cool for 10–15 minutes.

4. Reduce the oven temperature to 180°C and spread walnuts on another baking tray. Roast for 8 minutes, stirring and turning halfway through, or until deepened in colour. Remove from the oven and allow to cool.

5. Peel the skin off the capsicum and place the flesh into a food processor. Add the walnuts, garlic, lemon juice, cumin, smoked paprika, chilli powder and a pinch of salt and pepper. Process until smooth, stopping to scrape down the sides as needed.

6. Transfer the dip to a serving bowl. If you like, drizzle with olive oil and sprinkle with chopped walnuts.

small plates and snacks.

butter bean and artichoke dip.

SERVES 6   **PREP TIME** 10 MINUTES

400 g can butter beans, drained and rinsed
½ cup (115 g) drained marinated artichokes
2 tablespoons artichoke marinade (from the jar), plus extra if needed
1 clove garlic
¼ cup (70 g) tahini
juice of ½ lemon

TO SERVE (OPTIONAL)
olive oil and chilli powder

1. Place the butter beans, marinated artichokes, marinade, garlic, tahini, lemon juice and a pinch of pepper into a food processor. Process until smooth, adding a dash more artichoke marinade if needed to loosen.
2. Transfer the dip to a serving bowl. If you like, drizzle with olive oil and a sprinkle of chilli powder.

chunky pesto.

SERVES 6   **PREP TIME** 10 MINUTES

2 cups basil leaves
1 cup flat-leaf parsley leaves
¼ cup (40 g) pine nuts, toasted
¼ cup (60 ml) olive oil
1 clove garlic
juice of ½ lemon

TO SERVE (OPTIONAL)
olive oil

1. Combine the basil, parsley, pine nuts, olive oil, garlic, lemon juice and a pinch of salt and pepper in a food processor. Pulse on and off for 1–2 minutes, or until it reaches the desired consistency.
2. Pour the pesto into a jar. If you like, drizzle with olive oil.

small plates and snacks.

cashew queso.

GF OF RSF

SERVES 6   **PREP TIME** 10 MINUTES

½ (75 g) cup raw cashews
150 g silken tofu
⅓ cup (20 g) nutritional yeast
1 clove garlic
juice of ½ lemon
1 tablespoon tahini
⅓ cup (80 ml) soy milk, plus extra if needed
½ teaspoon ground turmeric
¼ teaspoon smoked paprika

TO SERVE (OPTIONAL)
ground turmeric

1. Soak cashews in boiling water for 10 minutes, then drain.
2. Combine the tofu, nutritional yeast, garlic, lemon juice, tahini, soy milk, ground turmeric, smoked paprika, cashews and a pinch of salt and pepper in a food processor. Process until smooth, adding an extra dash of soy milk if needed to loosen.
3. Pour the queso into a jar. If you like, sprinkle over turmeric.

coconut tzatziki.

GF OF RSF

SERVES 6   **PREP TIME** 5 MINUTES

½ Lebanese cucumber, grated
1 cup (240 g) coconut yoghurt
juice of ½ lemon
1 tablespoon olive oil
1 clove garlic, finely chopped.
1 tablespoon chopped dill
2 teaspoons chopped chives

TO SERVE (OPTIONAL)
chopped chives and chilli flakes

1. Line a bowl with cheesecloth and place the grated cucumber in the centre. Wrap the cheesecloth around the cucumber and squeeze to remove excess liquid.
2. Place the coconut yoghurt, lemon juice, olive oil, garlic and a pinch of salt and pepper into a large bowl and mix well.
3. Fold through the cucumber, dill and chives until well combined.
4. Transfer the coconut tzatziki to a serving bowl. If you like, sprinkle with chopped chives and chilli flakes.

simple cashew cream.

SERVES 6 **PREP TIME** 5 MINUTES

1 cup (150 g) raw cashews
juice of ½ lemon

SAVOURY AD-INS (OPTIONAL)
1 clove garlic
1 teaspoon dried herbs or spices

SWEET AD-INS (OPTIONAL)
2 tablespoons rice malt syrup
1 teaspoon vanilla extract

1. Soak cashews in boiling water for 10 minutes, then drain.
2. Place the cashews, lemon juice, ⅔ cup (160 ml) water and a pinch of salt into a food processor. Process until smooth, stopping to scrape down the sides as needed.
3. Add the savoury or sweet ad-ins, if using, and process until well combined.
4. Pour the cashew cream into a jar.

I meet the right people at the right time to learn the right lesson.

small plates and snacks.

seeded crackers and cheese.

SERVES 6 **PREP TIME** 30 MINUTES + 3 HOURS SETTING **COOK TIME** 1 HOUR

Just because vegans don't eat dairy doesn't mean they can't enjoy a cheeseboard! This is my go-to cheese and cracker recipe. It's a guaranteed way to impress guests at a dinner party when you tell them it's 100% vegan!

CHEESE
1 cup (150 g) raw cashews
juice of 1 lemon
¼ cup (15 g) nutritional yeast
2 tablespoons olive oil
1 teaspoon Dijon mustard
1 teaspoon garlic powder
½ teaspoon smoked paprika
¼ teaspoon onion powder
¼ teaspoon ground turmeric
1½ tablespoons agar agar powder

SEEDED CRACKERS
⅔ cup (100 g) chickpea flour
½ cup (70 g) pumpkin seeds (pepitas)
½ cup (75 g) sunflower seeds
¼ cup (35 g) sesame seeds
¼ cup (15 g) nutritional yeast
2 tablespoons flaxseeds
2 tablespoons chia seeds
½ teaspoon garlic powder
1 teaspoon dried rosemary
2 tablespoons olive oil

TIP

For the perfect cheeseboard, serve this cheese and crackers with fresh berries, dried fruit, vegetable sticks and your choice of one or two dips from the recipes above. This cheese is best stored in an air-tight container in the fridge for 3–4 days.

1. To make the cheese, soak the cashews in boiling water for 10 minutes, then drain. Grease an 800 ml bowl or ramekin.

2. Combine the cashews, lemon juice, nutritional yeast, olive oil, Dijon mustard, garlic powder, smoked paprika, onion powder, ground turmeric, a pinch of salt and pepper and ⅓ cup (80 ml) water in a food processor. Process until smooth.

3. Heat 1 cup (250 ml) water in a saucepan over medium heat. Add the agar agar powder and stir constantly until boiling. Boil for 1 minute and remove from heat. Add the cashew mixture and mix well. Quickly pour mixture into the greased ramekin. Cover and refrigerate for 2–3 hours, until set.

4. Meanwhile, to make seeded crackers, preheat oven to 175°C.

5. Place the chickpea flour, pumpkin seeds, sunflower seeds, sesame seeds, nutritional yeast, flaxseeds, chia seeds, garlic powder and dried rosemary into a bowl. Mix until well combined and make a well in the centre.

6. Pour in the olive oil and ⅓ cup (80 ml) warm water. Mix with your hands until a dough forms. Roll into a ball and place between two pieces of baking paper.

7. Using a rolling pin, roll the dough until about 3–4 mm thick. Remove the top layer of paper. Lift the dough on the bottom piece of paper onto a large baking tray.

8. Bake for 1 hour, or until golden and crisp. Remove from the oven, allow to cool for 10 minutes then break into shards.

9. To serve, invert the ramekin onto a plate. Carefully tap to release the cheese. If it doesn't come out straight away, try going around the edge with a knife to loosen. Serve on a platter with the crackers.

I make new friends who are aligned with me easily and frequently.

baked potato wedges with BBQ sauce.

SERVES 6   **PREP TIME** 10 MINUTES   **COOK TIME** 40 MINUTES

This is my healthy take on hot chippies! The wedges are oven-baked giving them a slightly crispy exterior and soft interior. They pair perfectly with my homemade BBQ sauce which is refined sugar free and takes 2 minutes to mix up.

WEDGES
2 tablespoons nutritional yeast
½ teaspoon smoked paprika
½ teaspoon garlic powder
½ teaspoon onion powder
9–12 white potatoes, cut into 4 wedges each
1 tablespoon olive oil

BBQ SAUCE
½ cup (140 g) tomato paste
1½ tablespoons balsamic vinegar
1 tablespoon tamari
1 tablespoon rice malt syrup
1 teaspoon Dijon mustard
¼ teaspoon garlic powder
¼ teaspoon onion powder

TO SERVE (OPTIONAL)
chopped flat-leaf parsley and sea salt flakes

1. For the wedges, preheat the oven to 220°C and line a large baking tray with baking paper.

2. Mix the nutritional yeast, smoked paprika, garlic powder, onion powder and a pinch of salt and pepper in a small bowl.

3. Place the potato wedges into a large bowl. Drizzle with the olive oil and toss to combine. Sprinkle over the seasoning mix and mix with your hands until the potatoes are evenly coated.

4. Arrange potatoes on the baking tray and roast for 35–40 minutes, turning halfway, until golden and crisp.

5. Meanwhile, to make the BBQ sauce, place the tomato paste, balsamic vinegar, tamari, rice malt syrup, Dijon mustard, garlic powder, onion powder and a pinch of salt and pepper in a small bowl. Mix until well combined.

6. Remove the wedges from the oven. If you like, sprinkle with parsley and a touch of sea salt flakes. Serve with the bowl of BBQ sauce.

TIP

Both the potatoes and BBQ sauce can be stored in the fridge for 4–5 days. The BBQ sauce is also delicious in burgers, wraps or as a marinade to tofu. To reheat the potatoes, line them on a lined baking tray and bake in the oven for 10 minutes, or until hot, at 200°C.

I am allowed to let go of friends and welcome new ones.

grilled satay skewers.

SERVES 6 **PREP TIME** 10 MINUTES + 20 MINUTES MARINATING **COOK TIME** 4 MINUTES PER BATCH

A delicious and easy-to-make appetiser for summer BBQs and dinner parties. These tofu skewers are covered in the most drool-worthy tahini and almond satay. Don't get me wrong, I love a good peanut satay, but I wanted to show you that you can switch it up with other nut and seed butters as well!

SATAY SAUCE
2 tablespoons tahini
2 tablespoons full-fat coconut cream (shake the can before opening)
1 tablespoon almond butter
1 tablespoon tamari
juice of ½ lime
2 teaspoons vegan yellow curry paste
¼ teaspoon garlic powder

SKEWERS
500 g extra-firm tofu, pressed for 5 minutes and diced

TO SERVE (OPTIONAL)
coriander, sesame seeds and lime wedges

1. For the satay sauce, place the tahini, coconut cream, almond butter, tamari, lime juice, curry paste, garlic powder and a pinch of pepper into a small bowl. Mix well.

2. To assemble, thread 4–5 pieces of tofu onto each of 6 skewers. Place the skewers into a plastic container and pour over half of the satay sauce. Rub with your hands to coat the tofu evenly. Marinate in the fridge for 20–30 minutes. Reserve the other half of the satay sauce for serving.

3. Heat a heated gill or ridged sandwich press. Place the skewers on the grill and close the lid. Cook for 3–4 minutes, or until golden with grill marks. Remove from heat.

4. To serve, stack the skewers on a plate. Pour over some extra satay, serving any leftovers in a bowl next to the skewers. If you like, sprinkle with coriander and sesame seeds and serve with lime wedges.

TIP

If you want to create a full meal with these skewers, I love serving them on flatbread with leafy greens and a dollop of coconut yoghurt.

I mingle with successful people daily.

small plates and snacks.

chuna mousse crostini.

SERVES 6   **PREP TIME** 20 MINUTES   **COOK TIME** 12 MINUTES

I was never a fan of canned tuna and you'll hear why later in the book. This chickpea tuna (chuna) mousse crostini, however, is brilliant. The seaweed (nori) and dill give it a fish-like umami flavour, whilst the crostini provide a much-needed crunch.

CROSTINI
1 baguette, thinly sliced
1 tablespoon olive oil

CHUNA MOUSSE
400 g can chickpeas, drained and rinsed
150 g extra firm tofu, pressed for 5 minutes
¼ cup dill sprigs
1 sheet nori, torn
juice of ½ lemon
2 tablespoons soy milk
1 clove garlic
1 tablespoon drained baby capers
1 tablespoon baby caper brine (from the jar)
1 tablespoon Dijon mustard
1 tablespoon nutritional yeast

TO SERVE (OPTIONAL)
dill sprigs, nori flakes and chilli oil

1. Preheat the oven to 200°C and line two baking trays with baking paper.

2. Arrange the baguette slices on the baking trays and brush both sides with olive oil. Bake for 10–12 minutes, turning halfway, or until golden and crispy.

3. Combine the chickpeas, tofu, dill, nori, lemon juice, soy milk, garlic, baby capers and baby caper liquid, Dijon mustard, nutritional yeast and a pinch of salt and pepper in a food processor. Process until smooth, stopping to scrape down the sides as needed.

4. To serve, top the baguette slices with the chuna mousse. If you like, garnish with dill, nori flakes and a drizzle of chilli oil.

TIP

This chuna mousse is also delicious as a sandwich filling or side to a nourish bowl. It is best stored in an air-tight container in the fridge for 2–3 days.

I choose who I spend my time and share my energy with wisely.

roasted carrots on whipped tofu.

SERVES 6   **PREP TIME** 20 MINUTES   **COOK TIME** 40 MINUTES

You'll want to dive into the sweet, caramelised goodness of roasted carrots, perfectly paired with the creamy, airy delight of whipped tofu! Whether you're cooking up a cosy dinner for two or hosting a dinner party for the holidays, this small plate will bring a burst of personality to any table.

ROASTED CARROTS
3 bunches (about 750 g) baby (Dutch) carrots, trimmed and peeled
1 tablespoon olive oil
½ teaspoon ground cumin
¼ teaspoon smoked paprika
¼ teaspoon garlic powder

WHIPPED TOFU
450 g extra-firm tofu, pressed for 5 minutes
⅓ cup (80 ml) soy milk, plus extra if needed
2 tablespoons olive oil
1 tablespoon white miso paste
juice of ½ lemon
1 clove garlic

TO SERVE
1 teaspoon finely grated lemon zest
¼ cup (30 g) pecans, chopped
¼ cup flat-leaf parsley leaves, chopped
2 tablespoons pomegranate seeds

1. For the roasted carrots, preheat oven to 200°C and line a baking tray with baking paper.
2. Place the carrots into a large bowl and drizzle over the olive oil. Add the cumin, smoked paprika, garlic powder and a pinch of salt and pepper. Toss to coat evenly.
3. Spread the carrots onto the baking tray and cook for 35–40 minutes, turning halfway, or until tender and caramelised. Remove from the oven.
4. Meanwhile, to make the whipped tofu, place the tofu, soy milk, olive oil, miso paste, lemon juice, garlic and a pinch of pepper into a high-speed blender. Blend until smooth and creamy, stopping to scrape down the sides as needed. Add a dash more soy milk if needed to thin it out a little.
5. To serve, spread the whipped tofu on a plate and stack the carrots on top. Sprinkle over the lemon zest, pecans, parsley and pomegranate seeds.

TIP

If you only have access to regular-sized carrots, they will still work. However, I recommend halving or quartering them lengthwise depending on how big they are.

I am strong and confident enough to push myself out of my comfort zone to make new friends.

salads and nourish bowls.

you are perfectly imperfect.

If being labelled a perfectionist was a badge of honour, I used to wear it with pride. All during my childhood and into my late teens, everyone knew me as one. Good grades? Always. The front row in ballet class? Yep. Constantly looking glamourous? Of course. I was fuelled by positive feedback and people acknowledging my work, so when things didn't go as planned, it would hit home hard. I'd feel like that pack of slimy spinach rotting in the back of your fridge. Wilted and whiny. I remember sitting in year 8 art class with a pimple, the size of Jupiter, smack bang between my eyebrows. I was sitting across from my high school crush and I couldn't bear to look at him. Every time he'd flirt with me, I would smile and laugh facing the opposite direction. I was afraid that if he saw my pimple he would think that I was anything less than perfect. To top it off, we got our grades back for a drawing project. To my disappointment, I got an 89%. One measly per cent off an A+. I clutched that grade to my chest for dear life before anyone, especially my crush, could see. 'Congrats,' said the voice across from me. He saw my grade. The universe might as well have ended there.

Perfectionism is the need for every aspect of our lives, down to the last 1%, to be perfect. From the outside, a perfectionist can look like an industrious and meticulous individual. But when we look a little closer, we can see that perfectionism stems from deep-seated feelings of inadequacy. It's a shield to mask our insecurities. We fear that if we aren't perfect, then we aren't enough. And if we aren't enough, then what are we? In today's world, self-worth issues are rife, and I am no stranger to them. The pervasive influence of social media, news and television exacerbates these struggles, bombarding us with ever-shifting ideals of beauty, success and perfection to compare ourselves with. At 14 years of age, I remember reading an article on the 'perfect' lunch for achieving the Victoria's Secret body: a salad of canned tuna, pickles, tomatoes, kale and a splash of apple cider vinegar as the dressing. Entranced by the idealised image of the Victoria's Secret models, the golden girls of my era, can you guess what I made for lunch that day? The slimy canned tuna paired with the acrid tang of apple cider had me gagging. The taste of that salad was far from perfect. Yet, I choked it down to try and attain the unattainable. That was the last time I touched a can of tuna. But it wasn't the last time I read a damaging article online that influenced my actions.

What it really boils down to is this: do you love yourself? Even when you don't look like a Victoria's Secret model, have a certain amount in the bank or have gardens maintained as well as Jane next door. Loving yourself does not have to be a narcissistic quality. You don't have to be like an influencer who tells everyone how many followers they have. That is not self-love, that is insecurity masquerading as confidence and ego. I'm talking about loving yourself because you are genuinely content and proud of who you are. You take care of your mind, body and soul because you value yourself and your well-being. You don't feel the need to broadcast your identity and achievements to the world because the only judgement that matters is your own.

If self-worth is a challenge for you, the first thing I recommend doing is filtering your social media feed. Follow accounts that uplift you, unfollow ones that don't. It's as simple as that. Reducing your screen time is also a must. I'm not going to lie and say that this is a strong suit of mine because it most definitely is not. I still struggle with maintaining a balance between time on and off my phone. But the longer we are on there, the more likely we are to fall victim to mindlessly scrolling through posts that breed gossip and negativity. To help with this, you can schedule downtime app limits through your phone's screen time settings, or if you work best with incentives, some screentime apps use reward-based systems depending on your goals.

Whilst social media can trigger feelings of insecurity, it's essential to recognise that it is not the root cause of them. Most of these struggles stem from childhood and early adult experiences. There is no straightforward answer that I can give you to overcome these challenges; however, I can recommend a few strategies that have worked for me:

1. **Be conscious of how you speak to yourself:** When you face yourself in the mirror each morning, what is the first thing you say to your reflection? What kind of language and tone do you use? The more critically you speak to yourself, the worse you will feel and the quicker you'll make a habit of it. Recognising this pattern and intercepting the negative self-talk is crucial for fostering a healthier relationship with yourself. Instead, aim to cultivate a habit of speaking kindly to yourself. This could involve offering encouraging thoughts during your workouts, patting yourself on the back when you accomplish a task, or even greeting your reflection in the mirror with a loud and proud 'Hey there, hottie' each morning. This is going to take conscious thought and effort. It might make you cringe or, better yet, it might make you laugh. But I can promise that it's much better than peeling open your eyes in the morning and mumbling 'ew'. The more we can speak from a place of love for ourselves, the more likely that over time we will begin to feel and believe it.

2. **Seek support:** This could be through leaning on family members or friends, or even paid support such as a therapist or life coach. I invested in a life coach at 19 and can confirm that it was one of the most rewarding investments I have ever made in myself. Having someone to whom you can speak regularly to offer encouragement when you are feeling a little rough can completely shift your perspective and uplift your spirit.

3. **Do the mindset work:** If I sound like a broken record, I'm sorry. But again, I'm going to tell you that practising gratitude, affirmations, goal setting and meditation will do wonders for all aspects of your life, particularly in bolstering self-worth. The way we feel about our lives is parallel to the way we feel about ourselves. By recognising the abundance in our lives, we concurrently nurture feelings of self-love and acceptance.

4. **Recognise your humanity:** I bet that even the most successful and affluent individuals to walk this Earth still have off days. It's simply part of being human. We are meant to experience a range of emotions, that is why we have them. On challenging days, when your self-worth is low, sometimes the best course of action is to simply sit with those feelings, acknowledge their presence and understand that it's okay to not feel okay. Attempting to inundate yourself with positive affirmations might even exacerbate how crappy you feel. Crying is a great way to release a bulk of emotion. So is screaming, dancing or punching a pillow. Finding healthy outlets for releasing pent-up emotions is key. I know that for myself, I like to play soft

music, stand in the shower and have a good cry. And by good cry I mean the type of cry you experience after watching *Titanic* for the first time. A boohoo on steroids. I've turned it into a ceremonial ritual, a farewell cry to all that no longer serves me. Then when I exit the shower, after losing a few kilograms of emotional weight to the drain, I sense a tangible shift. My negative stream of thought has, literally and figuratively, been washed away. Leaving space for new thoughts rooted in self-love and positivity to flow in.

Remember, the path to self-love is a continuous process and requires time and effort. But with each step taken, you'll be closer to embracing your authentic self with gratitude and compassion.

Within perfectionism, there is also an element of self-distrust. Have you ever turned a half-hour task into an all-day affair? It's like your efforts are never good enough so you become ensnarled in a cycle of endlessly refining and redoing your work. When I first started creating content, filming recipes became an exercise in excess. I would take shot after shot to make sure every angle of the final meal was perfect. Even a simple three ingredient recipe would take me hours to film because of how many 'just in case' shots I'd take. It was only when I reflected this to my life coach at the time that I was confronted with the simple but profound question: 'Why do you not trust yourself?'. Huh? Trust myself? Of course I do! I'm just a born perfectionist, it's practically coded in my DNA, I told her. Then she repeated the same question: 'Why do you not trust yourself?'

Ahhh, light bulb moment. The very act of filling up my camera roll with a thousand shots of the same thing was a sign that I didn't trust my ability to get the shot. More so, I didn't trust myself in general. The truth is, if you don't trust yourself from the start of a venture, you won't trust yourself at the end of it. That is, if you don't give up halfway anyway. It doesn't matter how long you try or if you are the most skilled professional in your field. If you don't trust your abilities, you'll fall into a self-perpetuating cycle of attempting to perfect every little detail and feeling stressed when you can't. Your self-distrust is preventing you from being happy and fulfilled. You might even find yourself constantly asking other people for their opinions on your work because you don't trust your own. God help my mum for the number of times I have pestered her to decide whether my work looked ok. When she would tell me it was great, I still wouldn't believe it. Sometimes I was so distrusting of my work that I began to rely on 'universal guidance'. And by universal guidance, I mean searching up a yes/no wheel online, spinning the wheel and waiting to see where it landed. No? Thank you, universe, I'll discard my work entirely. Chloe, that wasn't the universe. That was your own mind.

To rebuild self-trust, we must relinquish our need for perfection. There are two tools that I use to empower me to move through this that you might like to adopt yourself. One, set time limits. For example, I started giving myself three minutes to get the final shot of each recipe. It was hard. As soon as that three-minute timer would go off I would worry that I had missed the shot. But, after a while of doing this, I grew comfortable with it. I realised how capable I was to get the shot within that timeframe and continued to roll with it. Number two, know this: perfectionism doesn't exist. It's a false construct. What one person sees as perfect will differ from another's perspective. All that exists is you in this present moment. So, why let a false construct stop you from creating something that could help other people? If I had let self-distrust and the imperfection of my recipes stop me from posting online, imagine all the people who would miss out on being inspired to cook plant-based food. Imagine all the people who are missing out on your creativity and knowledge right this second. What is more important: being perfect or helping people?

Fact is, I am not perfect. Neither are you. Or your partner, best friend, parents, or even your favourite celebrity. But thankfully, none of us are born to be. We are born to be human. With all our charisma, uniqueness, nerve and talent (cheers, RuPaul). The more we recognise this, the more we can love and trust ourselves just as we are. That being, **perfectly imperfect**.

The following recipe chapter is dedicated to salads and nourish bowls. Not to worry, there aren't any Victoria's Secret tuna salad recipes in sight. Just a bunch of banging plant-based recipes to fill your bellies. Let each bite of these salads be a reminder that, like you, a salad doesn't have to be 'perfect'. You don't need to eat salads that are only high in this and low in that. And you most definitely do not need to eat a salad to have the perfect this or that. Let's just appreciate the damn salad for what it is. A big, beautiful bowl of colour, flavour, nutrients and, put simply, fuel. Bon appétit.

roasted eggplant with creamy slaw bowl.

SERVES 6   **PREP TIME** 30 MINUTES   **COOK TIME** 30 MINUTES

I'm always getting asked how to cook eggplant. In my opinion, the most delicious way of all is also the simplest. Using only olive oil, salt, pepper and garlic powder, the flavour and texture of this eggplant is spot on. You can then bring extra flavour and flair to the dish with added sides and sauces, such as the creamy cabbage slaw and a punchy whipped harissa tahini in this nourish bowl.

ROASTED EGGPLANT
⅓ cup olive oil
1 teaspoon garlic powder
3 eggplants, sliced into 1.5 cm rounds

CABBAGE SLAW
2 tablespoons tahini
2 teaspoons Dijon mustard
juice of 1 lemon
½ small green cabbage, julienned
2 zucchini, shaved into ribbons
3 spring onions, julienned
400 g can cannellini beans, drained and rinsed
1 red chilli, thinly sliced

WHIPPED HARISSA TAHINI
½ cup (70 g) tahini
1 clove garlic
juice of ½ lemon
3 teaspoons rose harissa
½ teaspoon smoked paprika

TO SERVE (OPTIONAL)
chopped spring onion, thinly sliced chilli and toasted sesame seeds

1. For the roasted eggplant, preheat oven to 200°C and line a baking tray with baking paper.
2. Combine the olive oil, garlic powder and a pinch of salt and pepper in a small bowl and mix well.
3. Arrange the eggplant slices on the baking tray. Brush the marinade over both sides of each slice and rub in with your hands to coat evenly. Roast for 30 minutes, turning halfway, or until golden and tender.
4. Meanwhile, for the cabbage slaw, place the tahini, Dijon mustard, lemon juice, 1 tablespoon water and a pinch of salt and pepper in a large bowl. Mix until smooth, adding more water if needed to thin. Add the cabbage, zucchini, spring onions, cannellini beans and chilli and toss with your hands to coat all the ingredients evenly. Set aside in the fridge.
5. To make the whipped harissa tahini, place the tahini, garlic, lemon juice, harissa, smoked paprika, ½ cup (125 ml) water and a pinch of salt and pepper into a food processor. Process until thick and smooth.
6. To serve, place a large dollop of whipped harissa tahini onto plates and spread with the back of a spoon. Top with cabbage slaw and roasted eggplant. If you like, top with extra whipped harissa tahini, spring onions, chilli and toasted sesame seeds.

TIP

If you aren't a fan of spice, feel free to omit the harissa from the whipped harissa tahini.

I love and accept myself just as I am.

salads and nourish bowls.

beetroot and cucumber bowl.

GF **RSF**

SERVES 3   **PREP TIME** 10 MINUTES

10 minutes is all you need to make this delicious beetroot and cucumber salad bowl. The base is a creamy beetroot and white bean whip, which is topped with a zesty cucumber salad. This is perfect for a hot summer's day when you need something light and fresh.

BEETROOT WHIP
400 g can cannellini beans, drained and rinsed
4 cooked baby beetroot (250 g from vacuum sealed pack)
1 clove garlic
2 tablespoons tahini
2 tablespoons nutritional yeast
2 teaspoons balsamic vinegar

CUCUMBER SALAD
juice of ½ lemon
1 tablespoon olive oil
4 large Lebanese cucumbers, shaved into ribbons
2 tablespoons dill sprigs, chopped

TO SERVE (OPTIONAL)
vegan feta, dill and olive oil

1. To make the beetroot whip, combine the cannellini beans, beetroot, garlic, tahini, nutritional yeast, balsamic vinegar, 2 tablespoons water and a pinch of salt and pepper in a food processor. Process until smooth, adding a dash more water if needed to thin.

2. For the cucumber salad, mix the lemon juice, olive oil and a pinch of salt and pepper in a large bowl. Add the cucumber and dill and toss to coat.

3. To serve, dollop the beetroot whip into shallow serving bowls and top each with the cucumber salad. If you like, top with vegan feta and dill and a drizzle of olive oil.

TIP

You can substitute the cucumbers with zucchini in this recipe if you prefer.

I am enough as I am, and I continue to grow and evolve each day.

salads and nourish bowls.

orange and sesame noodle salad.

SERVES 4 **PREP TIME** 30 MINUTES + 20 MINUTES MARINATING **COOK TIME** 10 MINUTES

Noodle salads are one of my favourite kinds of salads. Not only are they delicious and easy to make, but the healthy serve of carbs from the noodles will keep you feeling energised. The sweetness and zest of the orange in this salad is perfectly complemented by the nuttiness of the sesame dressing and the umami flavour of the miso and tamari.

MISO ORANGE TOFU
¼ cup (60 ml) freshly squeezed orange juice
2 tablespoons tahini
1 tablespoon white miso
1 tablespoon tamari
2 teaspoons sesame seeds
500 g extra-firm tofu, pressed and diced

SESAME DRESSING
⅓ cup (80 ml) tamari
2 tablespoons rice vinegar
2 tablespoons toasted sesame oil
1 teaspoon finely chopped ginger
1 tablespoon rice malt syrup

SALAD
180 g soba noodles
1 cup (160 g) edamame beans, cooked and shelled
1 large carrot, julienned
1 large cucumber, diced
2 oranges, peeled and chopped into chunks
2 spring onions, chopped
⅓ cup coriander leaves, chopped
¼ cup mint leaves

TO SERVE (OPTIONAL)
sesame seeds

1. To marinate the miso orange tofu, mix the orange juice, tahini, miso, tamari, sesame seeds and a pinch of pepper in a small bowl until smooth.

2. Place the diced tofu into a large container and drizzle over the marinade. Secure the container lid and shake to coat evenly. Set aside in the fridge for at least 20 minutes to marinate.

3. For the sesame dressing, place all the ingredients into a jar. Secure the jar lid and shake until well combined.

4. Meanwhile, to start the salad, bring a large saucepan of water to the boil. Add the soba noodles and cook for 4–6 minutes. Drain, rinse under cold running water and set aside.

5. Heat a pan over medium heat. Add the tofu and pour any remaining marinade in. Cook for 4–5 minutes, flipping regularly, until the tofu is golden. Remove from the heat.

6. To finish the salad, place the soba noodles, edamame beans, carrot, cucumber, orange, spring onions, coriander and mint leaves. Drizzle over the dressing and toss to combine.

7. To serve, divide the salad among serving bowls and top with the miso orange tofu. If you like, sprinkle with sesame seeds.

TIP

If you don't have soba noodles on hand, ramen or rice noodles also work well in this salad.

I choose to see through a lens of love and acceptance.

salads and nourish bowls.

falafel mezze bowl.

SERVES 3 **PREP TIME** 20 MINUTES **COOK TIME** 35 MINUTES

Have you ever seen those TikTok or YouTube videos where they showcase the death-row meals of famous criminals? Thankfully, I'm never going to find myself in that position. However, if I did, I would request a big and beautiful mezze platter. It would require large quantities of four glorious elements: chickpea falafels, a juicy Shirazi salad, fluffy pita bread and last, but not least, a bowl of hummus. So, inspired by my death row meal, here is my (to die for) falafel mezze bowl.

BAKED FALAFEL
400 g can chickpeas, drained and rinsed
½ small red onion, roughly chopped
1 clove garlic
1 cup flat-leaf parsley leaves
1 cup coriander leaves
2 tablespoons tahini
2 tablespoons flaxseed meal
2 teaspoons ground cumin
1 teaspoon ground coriander
juice of ½ lemon
1 teaspoon baking powder

SHIRAZI SALAD
1 large Lebanese cucumber, finely diced
2 truss tomatoes, finely diced
½ small red onion, finely diced
⅓ cup fresh mint, chopped
juice of ½ lemon
1 tablespoon olive oil

TO SERVE
3 pieces pita bread (of your choice)
¾ cup (190 g) roasted garlic hummus (page 53)

1. To make the falafel, preheat the oven to 180°C and line a baking tray with baking paper.

2. Place the chickpeas, onion, garlic, parsley and coriander into a food processor and process until well combined but still chunky. Add the tahini, flaxseed meal, cumin, coriander, lemon juice, baking powder and a pinch of salt and pepper. Process until smooth but with a bit of texture remaining.

3. Scoop out roughly 2 tablespoons of the mixture and roll into a ball. Flatten to create a disc shape and place onto the baking tray. Repeat with remaining mixture to make about nine falafel.

4. Bake for 30–35 minutes, turning over after 20 minutes, until browned. Remove from the oven and allow to rest for 5 minutes.

5. Meanwhile, to make the Shirazi salad, place the cucumber, tomato, onion and mint into a large bowl. Drizzle over the lemon juice and olive oil and season with a pinch of salt. Toss to combine.

6. To serve, divide the Shirazi salad, falafel and pita bread among shallow bowls. Top with a big dollop of hummus.

TIP

If you are worried that the falafels are going to break when you turn them over, set them aside for 5 minutes to firm up slightly. Turn over and pop back into the oven to finish cooking.

I release the need for perfection and embrace my imperfections with compassion.

 salads and nourish bowls.

roasted cauliflower bowl.

SERVES 4 **PREP TIME** 20 MINUTES **COOK TIME** 45 MINUTES

This recipe proves that the more sauce, the better! Sitting on a creamy butter bean and artichoke dip, drizzled in a smoky capsicum sauce, and topped with a chunky pesto, this roasted cauliflower flower bowl is, quite literally, a saucy sensation.

ROASTED CAULIFLOWER
⅓ cup (80 ml) olive oil
2 tablespoons nutritional yeast
1 teaspoon smoked paprika
½ teaspoon garlic powder
2 heads cauliflower, cut in half

CAPSICUM SAUCE
1 red capsicum, sliced in half
1 shallot, halved
2 cloves garlic, skin on
2 teaspoons olive oil
¼ cup (40 g) raw cashews
1 tablespoon tamari
1 tablespoon tahini
½ teaspoon smoked paprika
½ cup (125 ml) soy milk, plus extra if needed

TO SERVE
1 quantity butter bean and artichoke dip (page 55)
1 cup (85 g) snow pea shoots

TO SERVE (OPTIONAL)
chunky pesto (page 55), toasted pine nuts, sesame seeds and flat-leaf parsley

1. Preheat oven to 200°C and line two baking trays with baking paper.

2. For the roasted cauliflower, mix the olive oil, nutritional yeast, smoked paprika, garlic powder and a pinch of salt and pepper in a small bowl. Place the cauliflower onto a baking tray and rub in the marinade to coat evenly. Roast cut side down in the oven for 40–45 minutes, or until golden and fork tender.

3. For the capsicum sauce, arrange the capsicum, shallot and garlic on the second baking tray. Drizzle with the olive and season with a pinch of salt and pepper. Roast for 20–25 minutes, or until fork-tender and the capsicum has charred. Soak the cashews in boiling water for 10 minutes, then drain.

4. Transfer the roasted capsicum, shallot and garlic (squeeze from skin) into a food processor. Add the cashews, tamari, tahini, smoked paprika and soy milk and process until smooth. Add a dash more soy milk if needed. Pour into a jar.

5. To serve, dollop the butter bean and artichoke dip onto serving plates. Top each with pea shoots and roasted cauliflower. Drizzle over the capsicum sauce. If you like, top with a few teaspoons of chunky pesto, toasted pine nuts, sesame seeds and parsley.

TIP

In step 3, keep the capsicum around the edges of the baking tray and the shallot and garlic in the centre so that they all cook evenly.

I trust in my abilities and believe in my potential to create a life of purpose and meaning.

salads and nourish bowls.

mustardy potato salad.

SERVES 4   **PREP TIME** 30 MINUTES   **COOK TIME** 30 MINUTES

This is not a traditional potato salad, it's even better. The dressing is honestly good enough to drink from the jar. Plus, do you know anyone who doesn't like crispy roasted potatoes? Neither do I. That's why it's my go-to salad to take to BBQs or holiday celebrations.

ROASTED POTATOES
12 baby potatoes, halved
1 tablespoon olive oil
2 tablespoons nutritional yeast
¼ teaspoon garlic powder

CREAMY DRESSING
¼ cup (70 g) tahini
2 tablespoons Dijon mustard
juice of ½ lemon
1 tablespoon rice malt syrup
¼ teaspoon garlic powder

SALAD
1 Lebanese cucumber, finely sliced
6 small radishes, halved
2 large handfuls mixed salad leaves

TO SERVE (OPTIONAL)
chopped chives

1. For the roasted potatoes, preheat oven to 220°C and line a baking tray with baking paper.
2. Toss the potatoes, olive oil, nutritional yeast, garlic powder and a pinch of salt and pepper in a large bowl until well combined. Spread potatoes onto the baking tray and roast for 25–30 minutes, turning halfway, or until fork tender and crispy on the outside. Remove from the oven and allow to cool for 15 minutes.
3. Meanwhile, for the dressing, place the tahini, Dijon mustard, lemon juice, rice malt syrup, garlic powder, ¼ cup (60 ml) water and a pinch of salt and pepper into a small bowl. Mix until well combined and smooth.
4. To serve, toss together the cucumber, radishes, salad leaves and potato in a salad bowl. Dollop over the dressing and mix until evenly coated. If you like, sprinkle with chopped chives.

TIP

To make sure the potatoes stay slightly crisp and avoid going soggy, mix in the dressing just before plating up.

I don't need to change or fix myself to love myself.

polenta caprese salad.

SERVES 5 **PREP TIME** 30 MINUTES + 50 MINUTES COOLING AND SETTING **COOK TIME** 40 MINUTES

The magical thing about polenta is that when it cools, it firms right up. Meaning that you can slice it and bake it into crispy and creamy cubes of goodness. It makes for a hearty and delicious mozzarella substitute in this fresh caprese-style salad.

BAKED POLENTA
2 cups (500 ml) vegetable stock
270 ml can full-fat coconut milk
1⅓ cups (225 g) instant polenta
⅓ cup (20 g) nutritional yeast
1 teaspoon dried rosemary
1 teaspoon dried oregano
¼ teaspoon garlic powder
1 tablespoons olive oil

DRESSING
2 tablespoons olive oil
1 tablespoon white balsamic vinegar
½ teaspoon Dijon mustard
¼ teaspoon garlic powder
¼ teaspoon dried oregano

SALAD
4 truss or heirloom tomatoes, sliced
½ cup basil leaves
2 tablespoons vegan feta, crumbled
1 tablespoon pine nuts, toasted
1 tablespoon balsamic glaze

TIP
The baked polenta also makes good dippers for the capsicum and walnut dip or hummus in the small plates chapter.

1. To start the baked polenta, combine the vegetable stock, coconut milk and 2 cups (500 ml) water in a saucepan. Mix well and bring to the boil over high heat.

2. Reduce heat to medium and slowly pour in the polenta, whisking constantly. Add the nutritional yeast, rosemary, oregano, garlic powder and a pinch of salt and pepper. Cook for 1–2 minutes, stirring constantly, or until thickened. Remove from heat.

3. Pour the polenta into a lightly greased glass baking dish (28 cm x 20 cm) and smooth with the back of a spoon. Allow to cool for 20 minutes, then refrigerate for at least 30 minutes to firm up.

4. Meanwhile, for the dressing, combine all the ingredients in a jar and add a pinch of salt and pepper. Secure the jar lid and shake until well combined.

5. For the salad, lay the sliced tomatoes in a shallow bowl and pour over the dressing. Cover and set aside to marinate in the fridge.

6. To bake the polenta, preheat the oven to 220°C and line a baking tray with baking paper. Cut the set polenta into square slices (roughly 5 cm x 3 cm). Arrange on the baking tray and drizzle with the olive oil. Rub with your hands to coat evenly. Bake for 30–35 minutes, turning halfway, or until golden and crisp. Remove from the oven and allow to cool for 10 minutes.

7. To serve, arrange the marinated tomatoes, basil leaves and baked polenta on a platter. Top with the vegan feta and toasted pine nuts, and drizzle over the balsamic glaze.

I release the need for external validation and find validation within myself.

butter bean caesar.

SERVES 5   **PREP TIME** 15 MINUTES   **COOK TIME** 40 MINUTES

Caesar salad cops a lot of flak for being known as the 'unhealthy' salad. Let this recipe change your perception of it. It's just as creamy and tasty as the original, only it's plant-based and filled with wholefood ingredients.

SMOKY BUTTER BEANS
400 g can butter beans, drained and rinsed
1 tablespoon olive oil
1 tablespoon (15 g) nutritional yeast
½ teaspoon smoked paprika
¼ teaspoon garlic powder

CROUTONS
3 cups (135 g) diced sourdough or gluten-free bread
1 tablespoon olive oil

CAESAR DRESSING
1 cup (150 g) raw cashews
1 tablespoon baby capers
1 tablespoon baby caper brine (from the jar)
1 clove garlic
juice of ½ lemon
2 teaspoons Dijon mustard
2 teaspoons balsamic vinegar
2 teaspoons tamari

SALAD
3 heads baby cos lettuce, chopped
¼ cup flat-leaf parsley leaves, chopped

1. Preheat the oven to 180°C and line two baking trays with baking paper.
2. For the smoky butter beans, pat beans with paper towel to remove excess moisture. Combine in a bowl with the olive oil, nutritional yeast, smoked paprika, garlic powder and a pinch of salt and pepper. Toss to coat evenly and spread over one baking tray. Roast for 35 minutes, turning and stirring halfway, or until crunchy.
3. Meanwhile, for the croutons, spread the diced bread over the other baking tray. Drizzle over olive oil, season with a pinch of salt and pepper and toss with your hands. Roast for 15–20 minutes, or until golden and crunchy.
4. To make the dressing, soak the cashews in boiling water for 10 minutes, then drain. Place into a food processor with the baby capers and brine, garlic, lemon juice, Dijon mustard, balsamic vinegar, tamari, ½ cup (125 ml) water and a pinch of salt and pepper. Process until smooth. Add a dash more water if needed to thin.
5. To assemble the salad, place the lettuce, ⅔ of the butter beans and ⅔ of the croutons in a salad bowl. Drizzle over the dressing and toss to combine. Top with the remaining butter beans and croutons, and the parsley.

TIP

If preparing this salad ahead of time, keep the dressing separate until serving so that some crunch remains in the lettuce and croutons.

I value my true self more than I value the need to be perfect.

 salads and nourish bowls.

black rice and rocket salad.

SERVES 4 **PREP TIME** 15 MINUTES **COOK TIME** 30 MINUTES

Black rice boasts a nuttier flavour and chewier texture compared to white rice, making it an ideal complement to salads. I love that it doesn't go soggy, even if packed for a day at work. I've opted for a fresh balsamic dressing to flavour this salad, to complement the cumin-spiced chickpeas and sweet pomegranate seeds.

SALAD
1 cup (200 g) black rice
100 g baby rocket leaves
seeds of 1 small pomegranate
½ cup (60 g) pecans, chopped
3 spring onions, chopped

BALSAMIC DRESSING
¼ cup (60 ml) olive oil
2 tablespoons balsamic vinegar
2 teaspoons rice malt syrup
1 teaspoon Dijon mustard
juice of ½ lemon

SPICED CHICKPEAS
2 teaspoons olive oil
1 clove garlic
1 teaspoons ground cumin
400 g can chickpeas, drained and rinsed
1 tablespoon nutritional yeast

TO SERVE (OPTIONAL)
vegan feta

1. To start the salad, cook the rice in a large saucepan of boiling water for 30 minutes or until tender. Drain and allow to cool.

2. For the balsamic dressing, combine the olive oil, balsamic vinegar, rice malt syrup, Dijon mustard, lemon juice and a pinch of salt and pepper into a jar. Secure the lid to the jar and shake well.

3. Meanwhile, for the spiced chickpeas, heat the olive oil in a frying pan over medium heat. Add the garlic and sauté for 30–60 seconds, until fragrant. Add the cumin and cook for a further 30 seconds. Add the chickpeas and nutritional yeast and cook for 3–4 minutes, or until the oil has reduced and the chickpeas are hot and well coated.

4. To assemble the salad, place the rocket, black rice, spiced chickpeas, pomegranate seeds, pecans and spring onions in a bowl. Pour over the dressing and toss to combine. If you like, garnish with vegan feta.

TIP

To make this meal more budget-friendly, you can substitute the black rice with a cheaper rice variety such as basmati or brown.

I treat myself with the same love and care that I offer to others.

salads and nourish bowls.

tex mex salad.

SERVES 4   **PREP TIME** 20 MINUTES   **COOK TIME** 50 MINUTES

I like to think of this salad as a deconstructed burrito. It's got avocado, black beans, corn and lettuce. The only difference is that instead of a tortilla, we are using sweet potato as it adds bulk and a delicious roasted flavour to the salad to keep you feeling full and fabulous.

ROASTED SWEET POTATO
1 large sweet potato (600 g), sliced into 1 cm rounds
1 tablespoon olive oil
2 tablespoons nutritional yeast

PICKLED ONIONS
¾ cup (180 ml) white vinegar
1 teaspoon rice malt syrup
½ teaspoon salt
1 red onion, thinly sliced
½ teaspoon whole black peppercorns

SPICED CORN AND BEANS
400 g can black beans, drained and rinsed
400 g can corn kernels, drained and rinsed
1 tablespoon olive oil
1 teaspoon ground cumin
½ teaspoon ground coriander
¼ teaspoon smoked paprika
¼ teaspoon garlic powder
⅛ teaspoon onion powder

AVOCADO CREMA
½ cup (75 g) raw cashews
1 ripe avocado
⅓ cup coriander leaves
juice of 1 lime
1 clove garlic

SALAD
1 small head iceberg lettuce, chopped
1 cup cherry tomatoes, diced
1 red capsicum, sliced

TO SERVE (OPTIONAL)
coriander leaves

1. Preheat oven to 200°C and line two large baking trays with baking paper.

2. To make the pickled onion, combine the vinegar, rice malt syrup, salt and ¼ cup (60 ml) hot water in a small bowl. Mix well. Place the onion and peppercorns into a jar. Pour over the vinegar mixture, seal the lid, and set aside in the fridge for at least 15 minutes.

3. For the roasted sweet potato, place the slices into a bowl. Drizzle over the olive oil and season with nutritional yeast and a pinch of salt and pepper. Toss to combine. Arrange on a baking tray. Roast on the lower shelf for 45–50 minutes, or until golden and tender.

4. For the spiced corn and beans, place the black beans, corn kernels, olive oil, cumin, coriander, smoked paprika, garlic powder and onion powder into a large bowl. Toss to combine. Spread over the other baking tray and roast on the upper shelf for 35 minutes, or until slightly charred and some beans are beginning to crack.

5. For the avocado crema, soak the cashews in boiling water for 10 minutes, then drain. Place into a food processor with the avocado, coriander, lime juice, garlic, ¾ cup (180 ml) water and a pinch of salt and pepper. Process until smooth.

6. To assemble the salad, place the lettuce on the bottom of a salad bowl. Top with the cherry tomatoes, capsicum slices, spiced corn and beans and roasted sweet potatoes. Dollop the avocado crema on top and top with pickled onion. Garnish with coriander, if you like.

I speak to myself with kindness and compassion, nurturing a loving inner dialogue.

 salads and nourish bowls.

broccolini and crispy tempeh salad.

SERVES 4   **PREP TIME** 15 MINUTES   **COOK TIME** 30 MINUTES

I'm not a fan of tempeh. Not even in the slightest. However, I'm a big fan of this broccolini and crispy tempeh salad. There's just something about roasting it until it's crisp and tossing it with fresh veggies and herbs that subdues its odd flavour.

CRISPY TEMPEH
300 g tempeh
1½ tablespoons olive oil
juice of ½ lemon
2 tablespoons nutritional yeast
1 teaspoon vegetable stock powder

SALAD
1 cup (190 g) quinoa, rinsed and drained
½ cup basil leaves, chopped
⅓ cup mint leaves, chopped
¼ cup (40 g) roasted almonds, roughly chopped
juice of ½ lemon

PAN-FRIED BROCCOLINI AND PEAS
1 tablespoon olive oil
2 bunches broccolini, ends trimmed, each stem halved lengthways
200 g sugar snap peas, trimmed
1 clove garlic, finely chopped

TO SERVE (OPTIONAL)
dried chilli flakes and shaved vegan parmesan

1. To cook the crispy tempeh, preheat oven to 200°C and line a baking tray with baking paper.

2. Crumble the tempeh into small chunks. Place into a large bowl with the olive oil, lemon juice, nutritional yeast, vegetable stock powder and a pinch of salt and pepper. Mix well. Spread onto the baking tray and roast for 20–25 minutes, turning and stirring halfway, or until golden and crisp.

3. Meanwhile, to start the salad, place the quinoa into a large saucepan of boiling water and cook for 12 minutes, until tender. Drain well, fluff the grains with a fork and set aside.

4. For the pan-fried broccolini and peas, heat the oil in a frying pan over medium heat. Add the broccolini and peas and stir-fry for 4 minutes. Add the garlic and a pinch of salt and pepper and stir-fry for a further minute, or until the vegetables are tender yet crisp. Remove from heat.

5. Transfer the broccolini and peas to a large bowl and add the quinoa, crispy tempeh, basil, mint and roasted almonds. Drizzle over the lemon juice and toss to combine. If you like, top with chilli flakes and vegan parmesan.

TIP

To keep the tempeh as crispy as possible, toss with the other ingredients just before you are about to serve the salad.

I trust in my worthiness and know that I deserve all the good that comes my way.

budget recipes.

money is your buddy.

When I used to think about money, I would get a murky and twisted feeling in the pit of my stomach. Kind of like when you've just realised you've eaten out-of-date yoghurt. It's a waiting game to see whether your body will keep it down or bring it back up. Not fun. It would feel icky to open my bank account to spend it, just as it would feel icky to open my bank account to save it. After many years of trying to understand this, I realised the feeling was a result of my conscious and unconscious thoughts and beliefs about money. As I touched on in an earlier chapter, I didn't have much money growing up. For most of my childhood, mum and I lived in a small 80s-style rental. The stovetop didn't work properly so we used matches to light it and the sunspots dotted through the carpet would scratch my feet every morning as I got out of bed.

In saying this, I am not at all going to deny my privilege. I am a white, straight woman who was raised in a cosy regional town in Australia and I have always had access to fresh food, clothing, education and a roof over my head. I was also gifted with the most down-to-Earth, loving, strong and supportive mother in the world, which was (and still is) my greatest privilege of all. However, we are all human. We all form beliefs from our childhood and past experiences that impact us as adults regardless of our racial, financial or cultural background. These beliefs can either help us to thrive or they can be major barriers in our growth. And if you haven't picked up on it, my beliefs around money were holding me back big time.

How did I overcome this? Well, in short, I spent almost all the money I had. When we were coming out of lockdowns in Australia I decided, after a long year and a half, that I was sick of working for others. I dreamt of working for myself in the online content creation space. It's not as if I hated any of my previous jobs or had horrible bosses – in fact, I had a great mix of bosses. Some that supported me, others that challenged me, and one that made me laugh so hard every day that my ribs hurt. It was more the fact that I was ready to put my love, energy and passion into my own dream as opposed to someone else's. The only issue I faced was that I was too nervous to invest any money in myself and potentially leave the stable income of retail and social media marketing work. One night I saw a girl that I followed on Instagram talking about her powerful experience with a life coach. This girl was an inspiration to me. She had been working for herself since she was young, had a large online following and owned multiple businesses. I googled the life coach she hired and felt deflated when I saw that to work with her one-on-one was just under $6000, which, when you're 19 years old, working multiple casual jobs and have roughly $7000 worth of savings, seems like a lot of cash to splash. The next morning at work, my boss and I had a small argument, and, unlike my usual self, I spoke back, making the argument much bigger than it needed to be. Ten minutes later I was sitting in the bathroom, sobbing and sniffling like a blubbery mess. In the heat of the moment, I decided to fill in the online application form to work with the life coach one-on-one. What I wrote in that application form, I couldn't tell you. It's all a blur. The only box I clearly remember filling out with a big, nervous, shaking, cringing, stomach-crawling, heart-pounding yes was 'Do you have the financial capacity to invest in life coaching.' And that was it. The next day, I left my job, had my first call with the life coach and paid the money on the spot.

The next three months were some of the toughest I have ever endured financially and mentally, but among the greatest three months of my life. Using meditation, inner child work, journaling, visualisation, breathwork and having someone to lean on for support, I focused on breaking down all my limiting beliefs and forming new ones. In this chapter, I want to share what I learnt about money both during my time in coaching and every day since. However, I do want to preface things by saying that money is not everything. It is merely a tool that we can use to achieve more abundance in both our lives and the lives of others. I also understand that money might not be as big a barrier for you as it was for me. However, I believe that the following lessons I am going to share can be adapted to almost all areas of our lives, whether that be in careers, relationships or health.

Understand money is energy: Everything in the universe is energy. You, in your essence, are a walking, talking and money-spending bundle of vibrating atoms. When we toss money around, we aren't just swiping cards or passing bills, we are exchanging energy. Back in the day, before money as we know it existed, people traded goods and services directly. For example, exchanging fresh vegetables one picked from a garden for firewood another chopped down. It was raw energy being exchanged. Real blood, sweat and tears. In modern society, this energy is now in the form of that $20 note on your counter, credit card in your wallet or loose change clinking around in the bottom of your bag. The energy exchange is still the same, the only difference is that we now assign it a dollar value. Here's the kicker: our thoughts and feelings are also energy. If we are constantly doubting our worth or are scared to receive money for our labour, we will vibrate on that frequency and attract situations in alignment with that; such as your boss forgetting to pay you or a client being late on an invoice. Likewise, if we are constantly worried about spending money, we will vibrate on that frequency and attract situations where we need to spend more of it. Shifting your thoughts and feelings around money to thoughts of love and gratitude will energetically set you on the path to acquire more.

Know that money is love: Think about one of the best meals that you have ever eaten. An acai bowl from a local café or the saucy pasta you slurped in Italy. Close your eyes and relive that experience. Taste all the flavours and feel all the textures. Now open your eyes. Without money, enjoying that meal would have never been possible. Food costs money. For us to live our most abundant and adventurous lives, we require money. I'm not at all saying that you must earn a lot to make you happy. Monks have proved that money does not equal happiness time and time again. It does, however, give you more opportunities to invest in yourself. You can buy books to grow your brain, and you can buy a gym membership to grow your booty. Cowabunga! A lot of our hang-ups about money come from stories friends, family and the media have told us since we were young. As a kid, I believed that if you had a lot of money, you must be an as*hole. You must be corrupt to get away with it and reap the benefits of being a corrupt as*hole. This is completely and utterly false. Some of the wealthiest people I have met are also some of the kindest and most giving. If you haven't met many wealthy people yourself, because before 2021 I hadn't either, you only have to do a quick Google search to see that many of the world's wealthiest entrepreneurs are frequent charity donors. Money allows us to give. Since giving is a form of love, then how could money be anything less?

Build a strong relationship with money: I am in a close relationship with my money. For me, it's like keeping tabs on a good buddy, except the buddy is my bank account. I track every dollar that comes in and every buck that goes out. When we begin to see a flow of money, we can begin to express gratitude for receiving that money. I do this by writing the exact dollar value I receive in my gratitude diary every night. Then I close my eyes, tune into the feeling of love and repeat thank you in my head or out loud. The main goal here is to treat money with love. The kind of love you'd give to your buddy. When we give love to the money we receive, we start to believe we deserve that money. We grow comfortable with receiving. Trouble comes when we grow so comfortable with receiving this amount and this amount only, that we place a cap on our buddy. We aren't letting them grow. I struggled with this for so many years and the best advice I can give you is to start setting small money targets. A target that feels uncomfortable but still within the realm of believability.

Back in 2021, I had grown to 20,000 followers on Instagram and was averaging around $200 per Instagram post for sponsored content. When I shared this with other people in my field, I was constantly hit with the same response: 'You are undercharging yourself'. I knew they were right but every time I'd increase my rates and send them to a client, I was constantly told that they didn't have that budget, or, more commonly, they'd ghost me completely. Whilst I loved my work and put an incredible amount of passion into it, it felt icky jumping from a rate in the hundreds to a rate in the thousands as others suggested, and so I was attracting clients who also felt icky spending that sort of amount. Instead, I decided to make a smaller money target. I thought I'd double it and go from $200 to $400. It felt exciting, and most importantly, it didn't feel icky. I began visualising $400 contracts coming through, sending $400 invoices, and seeing $400 appear in my bank account. I even wrote up a fake email from a dream client stating they'd like to work with me for $400. A couple of weeks later, I had three new sponsorship deals, two at $400 and one at $800. The $800 contract was, in fact, the exact dream client. I had reached my money target, and I was on to the next.

Create multiple sources of income: People want to spend their money. Really, they do. Even you want to spend your money. Heck, that's why it exists in the first place. Did you buy a coffee, fill up your tank with petrol or go grocery shopping for the ingredients for a plant-based dinner today (I hope so)? Everyone wants to spend their money on things that they feel will benefit them. So, the real question is, why wouldn't they want to spend their money on you? If you first want to earn more in your current job, the first thing you need to do is accept that it's possible. Research wealthy and successful people in the same line of work as you. Google them and see how they got to that position. Search them up on Instagram and notice what they are interested in or how they spend their time. Seeing how it has worked for someone else not only shows that it's possible for you too, but you might discover some handy tips and tricks to implement into your work life. The next is to affirm and journal the living daylights out of it. Some of my favourite money and work affirmations are:

'People cannot wait to work with me.'
'People pay me abundantly for my work.'
'I am exactly what people are looking for.'
'People want to give me money.'

Then visualise it. Close your eyes, picture, and thank that money for appearing in your bank account. If you believe that you are at the top of your earning potential at your current job, look to your hobbies and see if there is space for monetisation there. I've always loved organising paperwork. An odd task, I know. But I love it because it requires little thought with lots of focus. You can get peacefully lost in it. When I was a teenager, I offered to tackle a friend's mountain of paperwork for some pocket money. They agreed and I had everything neatly filed in alphabetical order by the end of the day. Cha-ching! There is honestly a need for everything in this world. Successful entrepreneurs are successful because they expose a need and provide a product for it. Even when you didn't realise there was a need for the product in the first place. If you love creating pottery, how about selling some pieces at a local market on Sundays, teaching classes at night or posting tutorial videos online? If time is a constraint, how about seeing a financial advisor and investing small amounts of money into different avenues? Even if it's just a few bucks you could be building the bank whilst you snooze! I always recommend having as many income sources as possible, both active (such as pottery) and passive (such as investing) so the opportunity for manifesting more wealth is endless.

Begin healthy budgeting: There was a stage in my life where $10,000 was the most I could have in my bank account. It was like a psychological threshold and as soon as I'd hit that mark, I'd find something to splurge on. A cute jumper in the middle of summer or an extra pair of sunglasses because of an exciting two-for-one deal. And if I wasn't spending it on something stupid, an unexpected bill would bring it down for me. Like the time a lady reversed into the front of our car just as I made it to $10,600. Can you guess how much the insurance excess cost? Yep, $600. To get over this $10,000 hump, I had to figure out why it felt so icky to move on from this. When working with my life coach, I uncovered a deep-seated fear associated with receiving money, a fear intertwined with shame and inadequacy. Reflecting on my upbringing, particularly my high school years, I realised how self-conscious I was being a girl from a low-income background. I was lucky enough to get a scholarship to one of the top private schools in my area where most of the students came from money. Whilst I had a supportive group of friends I didn't like receiving help from them. I felt embarrassed that they had offered in the first place, so I would politely decline. Even when that meant taking a million photos of textbooks from the library because I couldn't afford to have copies of my own, and missing out on a few school camps and events. When I started earning money, it was still tied in with these feelings of shame. This feeling was particularly present when I would hit the $10,000 figure as I had never seen that many digits in my bank account, or any bank account for that matter, in my life. It felt uncomfortable and so subconscious impulses would drive me to spend it.

Resolving my limiting beliefs around money was one thing, which I used the lessons discussed above to do, but understanding and acknowledging where the heck my dosh was disappearing to all the time was another obstacle. The first time I went through my bank statement I was stunned. How on Earth did I manage to spend more on clothes in one week than I had spent on food in two months? Especially when I cook for a living! I'd even bought the most expensive vegan feta from my local grocer multiple times that month and still managed to spend considerably less on groceries than retail. No wonder my bank account couldn't stay at the five-digit mark.

So, I made a simple budget. I recommend you do too. Seeing exactly where your money is going gives you more control and clarity over your financial situation. You will be better informed to make decisions about where to spend it, just as you will be better able to set financial goals. Otherwise, it can feel as if you are blindfolded in the middle of Paris and getting pennies picked from your pocket. I understand that if you work for yourself, budgeting can be a bit trickier as your income isn't as consistent. I know for myself that some months can be more prosperous than others. In that case, I suggest calculating your average income from the past three months and using that figure.

Here is my go-to monthly budget formula:

- Calculate all the money you need for living and work expenses for the month. Such as rent/mortgage, gas, electricity, food, etc. Subtract that figure from your monthly budget.
- Whatever budget is remaining, divide it into two.
- Put aside half for savings and half for 'investing in yourself'. This investment could be getting a coffee with a friend, buying a new book, or attending a Pilates class. Sometimes, it could also be buying that new top that you can't stop thinking about (because you deserve to feel beautiful in the clothes you wear). Whatever feels in alignment with you for that month.

Obviously, we can't always stick to a strict budget. Unexpected costs can pop up and unexpected money can come in. Life happens. Don't beat yourself up about it. But the more we regularly track where it is going, the better opportunity we give ourselves to catch out spending habits that don't serve us and replace them with healthier ones.

Today, one of my biggest expenses is food. No surprises there. Not only is it part of my job, but I feel healthier and clearer when I spend an extra penny on higher-quality produce. However, that doesn't mean you have to. It is a misconception that healthy vegan dishes are expensive. Vegetables, grains such as rice and pasta, and protein sources such as tofu and legumes are the cheapest foods available in the supermarket. When cooked right, they can make for minimal-effort meals with complex flavours.

If food is an area you want to reduce your spending in, then welcome to budget meals. A chapter dedicated to breaking the stigma around the cost of plant-based food. Each recipe has a maximum of six budget-friendly ingredients for a delicious and nutritious lunch or dinner. Excluded from the six ingredients are pantry basics such as salt, pepper, olive oil and water. I've also added notes in the introduction and a tip section for each recipe if you'd like to add extra flavour or garnishes. I hope you and your buddy (the bank account) enjoy!

butternut pumpkin risoni.

SERVES 4   **PREP TIME** 10 MINUTES   **COOK TIME** 35 MINUTES

This book is a no-risotto zone. I've been scarred from watching too many MasterChef episodes where risotto, A.K.A the death dish, sent contestant after contestant packing for being too wet and clumpy. So, the most convenient solution is risoni. Or as I like to think of it, pasta in the shape of rice. It's much easier to cook and pairs well with a simple butternut pumpkin sauce.

½ a butternut pumpkin (900 g), peeled, seeded and cut into 2 cm cubes
½ brown onion, cut in half
2 cloves garlic, skin on
1 tablespoon olive oil
250 g risoni
2 tablespoons tahini
1¼ cups (310 ml) soy milk

1. Preheat oven to 200°C and line a large baking tray with baking paper.
2. Place the butternut pumpkin, onion and garlic into a large bowl. Add the olive oil and toss to coat evenly. Spread onto the baking tray and roast for 30 minutes, turning halfway, or until golden and tender. Remove from the oven and reserve about 1 cup of the roasted pumpkin for serving.
3. Meanwhile, bring a large pot of water to the boil. Add the risoni and cook according to package instructions until 3 minutes before al dente. Drain, reserving 1 cup (250 ml) pasta water and return to the pot.
4. Squeeze the garlic cloves out of their skin and place into a food processor with the onion, remaining pumpkin, tahini, soy milk, pasta water and a pinch of salt and pepper. Process until smooth.
5. Pour into the pot with the risoni and cook over medium heat for 2–3 minutes or until hot and sauce has thickened.
6. To serve, scoop into serving bowls and top with the reserved roasted pumpkin.

TIPS

For extra flavour, feel free to add a pinch of dried sage or smoked paprika into the food processor in step 4. I also love to garnish with olive oil and fresh sage.

Money comes to me easily and frequently.

sweet potato and rice tray bake.

SERVES 4   **PREP TIME** 10 MINUTES   **COOK TIME** 45 MINUTES

Tray bakes are the ultimate lazy dinner. Basically, you throw everything onto a baking tray, wrap it in foil and bake it in the oven. The combination of curry paste and coconut milk gives this tray bake so much flavour and considering it only has five ingredients, it's also budget-friendly.

2 sweet potatoes (1 kg), pre-diced into 1 cm cubes
2 cups (240 g) frozen peas
1 cup (200 g) medium grain rice
400 ml can full-fat coconut milk
1½ tablespoons vegan yellow curry paste

1. Preheat the oven to 180°C and grease a baking dish (roughly 41 cm × 32 cm × 3.5 cm).
2. Spread the sweet potato and frozen peas onto the tray and scatter with the rice.
3. Combine the coconut milk, 1 cup (250 ml) water, curry paste and a pinch of salt and pepper in a jug. Mix well. Pour into the tray and stir so that all the ingredients are covered.
4. Cover tray tightly with foil and bake for 45 minutes, or until the sweet potato is tender and the rice has absorbed all the liquid.
5. Remove from the oven and serve.

TIP

You can substitute the sweet potato for other root vegetables such as potato, pumpkin or even carrots depending on the most budget-friendly option available to you. Optionally, garnish with spring onion if you have any on hand.

I am worthy of financial freedom.

mujadara inspired salad.

SERVES 4   **PREP TIME** 15 MINUTES   **COOK TIME** 35 MINUTES

Mujadara is a traditional Middle Eastern dish made of lentils, rice and crispy onions, making it incredibly budget-friendly. To bump up the nutrient profile and add some colour, I've added fresh rocket to make this more of a salad-style recipe.

⅓ cup (80 ml) olive oil
2 brown onions, halved and sliced
5 cups (1.25 litres) vegetable stock
2 cups (400 g) dried brown lentils
1 cup (200 g) long-grain white rice
2 teaspoons ground cumin
150 g cups baby rocket

1. Heat the olive oil in a large frying pan over high heat. Add the onions and cook for 20 minutes, stirring often, or until brown and crisp at the edges. Transfer to a large plate lined with paper towel and allow to cool and crisp further.

2. Meanwhile, combine the vegetable stock and lentils in a large saucepan. Bring to the boil over high heat. Reduce heat to low and simmer, covered, for 15 minutes. Stir in the rice and cook, covered, for another 15–20 minutes, until the lentils and rice have absorbed the stock and are tender.

3. Remove from heat and allow to cool, uncovered, for 10 minutes . Fluff the rice and lentils with a fork and mix in the cumin and a pinch of salt and pepper.

4. To serve, place a bed of rocket into a shallow bowl. Top with the rice and lentil mix and garnish with the crispy onions.

TIP

For some crunch, feel free to sprinkle some fresh nuts on top such as pistachios, almonds or walnuts if you have any on hand.

I am at peace with working hard to make money.

easy lentil bolognaise.

SERVES 4   **PREP TIME** 10 MINUTES   **COOK TIME** 55 MINUTES

A basic bolognaise was one of the first recipes I learned to make as a child with mum in the kitchen for three reasons. One, it's incredibly cheap. Two, it's dead easy. And three, who doesn't love pasta? For extra flavour, garnish with fresh herbs such as basil or parsley if you have any on hand.

1 tablespoon olive oil
½ brown onion, finely diced
1 clove garlic, finely chopped
1 cup (200 g) dried brown lentils
700 ml herbed tomato passata
2 tablespoons balsamic vinegar
300 g pasta (of your choice)

1. Heat the olive oil in a large saucepan over medium heat. Add the onion and sauté for 3–4 minutes, or until translucent. Add the garlic and a pinch of salt and pepper and cook for a further minute.
2. Add the lentils and 4 cups (1 litre) water. Bring to the boil and then reduce heat to low. Simmer, partially covered, for 25–30 minutes, or until the lentils are al dente.
3. Add the passata and balsamic vinegar. Mix well and cook for a further 17–20 minutes, uncovered, or until thickened. Remove from heat.
4. Bring a large pot of water to the boil. Add the pasta and cook according to package instructions until al dente. Drain well.
5. Divide the pasta among bowls and top with the bolognaise sauce. Mix and serve.

TIPS

To bump up the nutrient profile, you could also add some vegetables and 1 tbsp (30 g) nutritional yeast to this bolognaise. My go-to vegetables are peas and spinach, added at step 3.

I embrace different avenues and opportunities for income.

budget recipes.

curried chickpea jacket potatoes.

SERVES 2   **PREP TIME** 10 MINUTES   **COOK TIME** 1 HOUR

Potatoes and canned beans are some of the cheapest whole foods that you can buy at the supermarket. So, I've brought them together in this cosy and comforting ensemble of curried chickpeas on roasted potatoes. I love serving this meal with a dollop of coconut yoghurt, a wedge of lemon and fresh coriander if you have some on hand.

2 white potatoes (440 g), scrubbed and dried
1 tablespoon olive oil
1 clove garlic, finely chopped
⅓ cup (95 g) tomato paste
2 tablespoons tahini
1½ teaspoons vegan curry powder
400 g can chickpeas, drained and rinsed

1. Preheat the oven to 220°C and line a baking tray with baking paper.
2. Place potatoes on baking tray. Pierce each potato with a fork six times and drizzle over 2 teaspoons of olive oil. Roast for 55–60 minutes or until fork-tender with crisp skin.
3. Meanwhile, heat the remaining olive oil in a frying pan over medium heat. Add the garlic and sauté for 30–45 seconds, until fragrant. Stir in the tomato paste, tahini, curry powder and 2 tablespoons water and cook for a further 1–2 minutes or until thickened.
4. Add the chickpeas and a pinch of salt and pepper and mix well. Cook for 2 minutes or until heated through. Remove from heat.
5. Slice a cross into the top of each potato and squeeze to open. Fill with the curried chickpeas.

TIP

I recommend roasting the potatoes on the top or centre rack of your oven for crisper skin.

I align my spending with my values and priorities, ensuring financial harmony.

simple tofu curry.

SERVES 4 **PREP TIME** 10 MINUTES **COOK TIME** 20 MINUTES

This is the easiest curry in existence that, surprisingly, packs heaps of flavour and protein. For extra creaminess, you can top with coconut yoghurt. It's also delicious served with naan bread.

1 tablespoon olive oil
1 clove garlic, finely chopped
1½ tablespoons vegan curry powder
¼ cup (70 g) tomato paste
400 ml can full-fat coconut milk
450 g extra-firm tofu, pressed and diced
1 cup (200 g) long-grain rice

1. Heat the olive oil in a deep frying pan or pot over medium heat. Add the garlic and cook for 30–45 seconds, until soft. Stir in the curry powder and a pinch of salt and pepper and cook for 30 seconds, or until fragrant.

2. Add the tomato paste, coconut milk, 1 cup (250 ml) water and tofu and mix well. Cook, uncovered, for 15 minutes, stirring regularly, or until the curry has thickened. Remove from heat.

3. Meanwhile, cook the rice in a saucepan of boiling water for 12 minutes or until tender. Drain well.

4. To serve, divide rice among serving bowls and top with the curry.

TIP

For some greens, you can add a few handfuls of spinach during the last two minutes of cooking and stir until wilted then garnish with coriander leaves.

I am open to receiving all the wealth the universe brings me.

garlicky potato soup.

SERVES 3 **PREP TIME** 10 MINUTES **COOK TIME** 50 MINUTES

A thick and creamy potato soup that packs a robust punch from the garlic. You'll want to slurp it every night, with one exception. First dates . . .

4 white potatoes (880 g), peeled and cut into 4 wedges
2 tablespoons olive oil
1 small brown onion, diced
6 cloves garlic, peeled
1½ cups (375 ml) soy milk, plus extra if needed
2 cups (500 ml) vegetable stock
1 teaspoon dried thyme

1. Preheat the oven to 220°C and line a baking tray with baking paper.
2. Arrange potatoes on the baking tray, drizzle over 1 tablespoon of olive oil and rub in with your hands to spread. Roast for 35–40 minutes, turning halfway, until golden.
3. Meanwhile, heat olive oil in a saucepan over medium heat. Add the onion and sauté for 6–8 minutes, or until golden. Add the garlic cloves and potato and sauté for a further 3 minutes or until the garlic is golden and tender.
4. Add the roasted potatoes, onion and garlic mixture, soy milk, vegetable stock, dried thyme and a pinch of salt and pepper to a high-speed blender. Blend until smooth, adding a dash more soy milk if needed to thin.
5. Pour into a saucepan and cook for about 5 minutes over medium heat to heat up and slightly thicken. Divide among bowls and serve.

TIP

A good soup needs a good dipper. I recommend serving with a thick slice of toasted sourdough or whatever bread you have on hand. For extra flavour, I also love garnishing with olive oil and fresh herbs.

People want to pay me abundantly for my work.

miso carrot pasta.

SERVES 4 **PREP TIME** 10 MINUTES **COOK TIME** 45 MINUTES

Carrots are one of the most budget-friendly vegetables in the supermarket and they just happen to make a beautiful base for pasta sauces. This carrot pasta is slightly sweet, slightly salty and super comforting. If you have any fresh herbs or nuts lying around, sprinkle them on top for extra crunch and colour.

4 carrots (260 g), chopped into 2 cm thick slices
½ brown onion, quartered
2 garlic cloves, peeled
1 tablespoon olive oil
500 g pasta (of your choice)
¼ cup (70 g) tahini
1½ tablespoons white miso paste

1. Preheat the oven to 200°C and line a baking tray with baking paper.

2. Spread the carrots, onion and garlic onto the baking tray and drizzle over the olive oil. Roast for 25 minutes, then remove the onion and garlic from the tray. Roast the carrots for a further 20 minutes or until slightly charred and tender.

3. Meanwhile, bring a large saucepan of water to the boil. Add the pasta and cook according to package instructions until al dente. Drain the pasta, reserving 2 cups (500 ml) of pasta water, and set aside.

4. Combine the roasted carrots, onion, garlic, tahini, miso paste, reserved pasta water and a pinch of salt and pepper in a high-speed blender. Blend until smooth, adding a touch more water if needed to thin.

5. Pour the carrot sauce into a large saucepan and bring to a simmer over medium heat. Cook for 1–2 minutes, or until thickened slightly. Mix in the pasta to heat through and serve.

TIP

For more flavour, you can add ¼ teaspoon smoked paprika and ¼ cup (15 g) nutritional yeast to the sauce if you have any on hand.

Money is an energy of love. I love money and money loves me.

tray bake tacos.

SERVES 4 **PREP TIME** 10 MINUTES **COOK TIME** 40 MINUTES

Butternut pumpkin is an easy and relatively cheap way to add bulk to meals. It's perfect in tray bakes and even better in tacos. To add some spice and a touch of creaminess to these tacos, you can add some chilli sauce, avocado slices or a dollop of coconut yoghurt on top if you have any on hand.

750 g butternut pumpkin, peeled, seeded, and cut into 1cm cubes
2 × 400 g cans black beans, drained and rinsed
400 g can diced tomatoes
2 teaspoons Cajun seasoning
8 corn tortillas
½ iceberg lettuce, chopped

1. Preheat the oven to 180°C and grease a baking tray (roughly 41 cm × 32 cm × 3.5 cm).
2. Spread the butternut pumpkin and black beans onto the tray. Mix the diced tomatoes, Cajun seasoning and a pinch of salt and pepper in small bowl. Pour into the tray and mix so that all the ingredients are covered.
3. Cover tray tightly with foil and bake for 40 minutes, or until the butternut pumpkin is tender.
4. Meanwhile, heat a frying pan over medium heat and toast the tortillas for 1–2 minutes on each side, until golden brown.
5. To serve, top the toasted tortillas with lettuce and the pumpkin and bean mixture.

TIP

If you prefer hard taco shells, feel free to substitute them for the tortillas in this recipe.

I am in control of my finances. I choose to create healthy budgets and stick to them.

couscous and sun-dried tomato salad.

SERVES 3   **PREP TIME** 10 MINUTES   **COOK TIME** 2 MINUTES + 10 MINUTES STANDING

In Australia, you can usually buy a box of dry couscous for somewhere around the $2 mark. Considering that you won't even use half the box in this recipe, I'd consider that a straight-up bargain. By using the marinade for the sun-dried tomatoes as the salad dressing, you are also reducing food waste!

¼ cup (310 ml) vegetable stock
2 tablespoons olive oil
1 cup (200 g) couscous
400 g can chickpeas, drained and rinsed
3 handfuls baby rocket
½ cup (75 g) drained marinated sun-dried tomatoes
2 tablespoons sun-dried tomato marinade (from the same jar)
1 Lebanese cucumber, diced

1. Combine the vegetable stock and 1 tablespoon of the olive oil in a saucepan. Bring to the boil.

2. Meanwhile, heat remaining 1 tablespoon of olive oil in a frying pan. Add the couscous and toast for 1–2 minutes, stirring constantly, until golden.

3. Transfer the couscous into the boiling vegetable stock, stir to combine then turn off the heat. Cover and stand for 10 minutes, or until the couscous has absorbed the stock. Uncover and fluff up the grains with a fork.

4. Place the couscous, chickpeas, rocket, sun-dried tomatoes and marinade, cucumber and a pinch of salt and pepper into a large bowl. Toss well to combine and serve.

TIP

For extra flavour, you could also add some flat-leaf parsley, mint leaves or diced red onion to this salad.

I invest money into things that will help me to grow.

sweet potato and capsicum soup.

SERVES 4 **PREP TIME** 10 MINUTES **COOK TIME** 40 MINUTES

This recipe is my most viral recipe on Instagram, with the reel currently sitting at a whopping 19.2M views. So, naturally, I had to include it in my first cookbook! It's easy, punchy and the Thai red curry paste gives it the perfect amount of spice. Garnish with some coconut yoghurt, chilli flakes and fresh coriander if you have any on hand.

1 red capsicum, sliced
1 tablespoon olive oil
1 large sweet potato (600 g), peeled and cut into 2 cm cubes
270 ml can full-fat coconut milk
1½ tablespoons vegan Thai red curry paste
400 g can chickpeas, drained and rinsed
1 clove garlic, finely chopped

1. Preheat oven to 200°C and line a baking tray with baking paper.
2. Spread the capsicum onto the baking tray, drizzle over 2 teaspoons of olive oil. Roast for 20–25 minutes, or until tender and slightly charred.
3. Meanwhile, place the sweet potato into a saucepan of water (enough to cover the sweet potato) and bring to the boil. Reduce heat to medium and cook for 15 minutes, or until tender. Remove from the heat and drain.
4. Combine the roasted capsicum, cooked sweet potato, coconut milk, red curry paste, 2 cups (500 ml) water and a pinch of salt and pepper in a food processor. Process until smooth.
5. Heat remaining 2 teaspoons of olive oil in a saucepan over medium heat. Add the chickpeas and garlic and sauté for 1–2 minutes, until fragrant.
6. Stir in the sweet potato and capsicum mixture. Reduce heat to medium-low and simmer for 10–15 minutes, stirring regularly, or until the soup has thickened. Remove from the heat.
7. Spoon into bowls and serve.

TIP

If you'd like to add more flavour, I recommend adding ½ brown onion, diced and sauteed for 2–3 minutes before sauteing the garlic and chickpeas, and replacing the water with vegetable stock.

I trust that I have more than enough money to meet my financial obligations.

roasted veg on whipped tahini.

SERVES 3   **PREP TIME** 10 MINUTES   **COOK TIME** 40 MINUTES

Colourful, fresh and budget-friendly! These delicious slices of roasted butternut squash with crispy lentils and kale on a bed of whipped tahini make for a nutrient-rich and low-effort meal.

½ butternut pumpkin (750 g), peeled, seeded and cut into 1.5 cm thick slices
¼ cup (60 ml) olive oil
400 g can lentils, drained and rinsed
1 bunch kale, stems trimmed, roughly chopped
1 teaspoon garlic powder
½ cup (140 g) tahini
juice of 1 lemon

1. Preheat the oven to 220°C and line two baking trays with baking paper.
2. Spread the pumpkin slices over one baking tray. Drizzle over 1 tablespoon of olive oil and rub in with your hands to coat the slices evenly. Season with a pinch of salt and pepper and roast for 35–40 minutes, turning halfway, or until tender and slightly charred.
3. Line a plate with a clean tea towel. Spread the lentils over the tea towel and pat dry with a separate tea towel. Transfer the lentils to the second baking tray, toss with 1 tablespoon of olive oil and push to one side of the tray.
4. Spread the kale on the other side of the baking tray. Drizzle over remaining 1 tablespoon of olive oil and toss to coat evenly. Season both the lentils and kale with ¼ teaspoon garlic powder and a pinch of salt and pepper each. Add to the oven to roast for the last 10 minutes of the pumpkin cooking time, stirring both sides halfway through, or until both are crisp.
5. Meanwhile, combine the tahini, lemon juice, ½ tsp of garlic powder and ½ cup (125 ml) water in a food processor. Process until thick and smooth.
6. To serve, spread the crispy kale on a plate and top with the roasted pumpkin. Dollop over the whipped tahini and garnish with the crispy lentils.

TIP

I recommend serving with a wedge of lemon if you have any on hand.

I use money to better my life and the lives of those around me.

quick dinners.

fear is wasting your time.

How much time do you waste every day? Really, how much? If you think that you don't waste a second, then you might as well close this book and stop reading here. I am almost certain that if you checked your phone screen time, you'd have at least one hour in front of you. Perhaps scrolling through your previously watched shows on Netflix would provide a few more hours. The 'I have no time' excuse is getting old and it's getting boring. When we really want to do something, we just do it. Ever had a deadline on a task that seemed impossible and somehow, because you knew you had to, you pulled it off? Even if that meant pulling an all-nighter and missing out on the next episode of *Love Island*. You did it because it was a must, and you dedicated all your time to it. But then another task comes around, and although you'd like to, you never seem to have enough time to get it done. Well, there are two simple reasons for this. Number one is when you do actually want to do the task, but fear is getting in the way. This fear is usually masked by procrastination. Number two, you don't actually want to do the task, but you think you should. If it's a should, then it's a could, which is a won't. You could cook a healthy meal, but you want to get a massage instead. You could go to the gym, but you want to call your friend instead. You could dedicate time to this, but you won't because it's not a priority.

FEAR

Let's explore number one first, fear. My modelling journey began when I was 19, but it wasn't without hurdles. At 18, I mustered up the courage to apply to two modelling agencies, only to face rejection from both. This was a major kick to the guts and especially to my teenage ego. Despite my interest in one other agency, the fear of getting knocked back a third time paralysed me. Each day I'd wake up with the intention of applying, only to find myself procrastinating until the day's end, drowning in a sea of excuses. I'd tell myself I couldn't apply yet because my regrowth needed touching up at the hairdresser. Or, I needed a more accurate tape measure to measure my height. Best of all, I needed to take my application photos outside where it just so happened to be bucketing down rain, so would have to wait until a sunny day. A year passed, along with many sunny days, and still, I hadn't applied. It took me having a big fat cry and a lengthy heart-to-heart with mum to accept the truth: it wasn't my hair, the tape measure, or the rain holding me back, it was my fear of rejection. Plain and simple. That night I finally submitted the application form and a day later I received an email expressing interest from the agency. A mere two weeks later I had signed with them and landed my first major modelling gig with Gorman, propelling me into the Melbourne fashion scene.

Procrastination and excuses only serve to waste time. When we avoid actions that are crucial for our growth, be it in our careers, relationships, finances or health, and instead find ourselves procrastinating, we must ask ourselves: what are we truly avoiding? What is it about completing this task that makes us feel scared, uncomfortable or insecure? Perhaps it's a fear of judgement, rejection, loss, pain, success or wealth. The longer we evade these truths, the more time we waste and the farther we stray from achieving our goals. The only way you are ever going to overcome fear is by facing it head-on. There is never going to be a right or wrong time to face your fears, so you might as well start now.

When I was a child, I used to love the book *We're Going on a Bear Hunt* by Michael Rosen. Whilst the book is about a family quite literally going on a bear hunt through long grass, cold rivers and thick mud, the book is actually a metaphor for overcoming obstacles.

And just as the bears confront their fears head on, so must we. The first step in this process is to uncover exactly what you fear. Begin by opening a journal or notepad and jotting down all the reasons why you *can't* have what you want. Yes, I said *can't*. There is often a common theme amongst your excuses that will help you uncover what's holding you back. For example, if you believe you can't meet the partner of your dreams because you aren't attractive, smart or wealthy enough, then what you really fear is judgement (side note – if someone genuinely likes you, they won't care whether you have three dollars or three million in your bank account). Write the corresponding fear next to each excuse so you can acknowledge it. Thank it for protecting you up until this point. But, let it know it's now time to disappear as it no longer serves you. Cross out each excuse and fear and next to it write a reverse excuse. That is, using the original excuse as a reason why you *can* achieve your goals. Here are some examples:

'~~I can't cook vegan meals because my family won't like them~~.' to 'I *can* cook vegan meals as I am in charge of my own diet and health. My family wants to see me well and nourished, and they love trying the leftovers.'

'~~I can't work in my dream field because I'm not smart enough~~.' to 'I *can* work in my dream field as I am intelligent, passionate and creative.'

'~~I can't go for a run this morning because I don't have enough time~~.' to 'I *can* go for a run this morning because I will wake up early enough to schedule it in.'

As I discussed in the first chapter, affirmations can be an incredibly powerful tool when repeated daily. You can use your reverse excuses as new affirmations to empower you to move through fear. When we stop wasting time, use affirmations and face our fears, we realise how ridiculous they were in the first place. They are purely fabrication. Think of how many hypothetical scenarios you have recited in your mind versus how many of them have eventuated. Probably very few. Fear also never exists in the present. If someone places a ticking bomb in front of you, you don't fear the bomb itself, you fear being blown up when that bomb goes kaboom. This is a gentle reminder that living in the present is a sure way to overcome fear.

Now, let's just say you take the action you have been avoiding through procrastination and it doesn't go as planned. Your fear comes to fruition. Your rental application gets knocked back. You lose a couple hundred smackaroos on an investment. You confessed your love to your crush who doesn't feel the same way. Dang nabbit. Yes, it's initially going to feel like crap. You might even want to shed a few tears. But, guess what? If you feel like crap, you're still alive. You've come out standing on the other side of that long grass, cold river and thick mud. What this means is that the universe has a better plan in store for you. Back when I was working with my life coach, she suggested that this might be for one of three reasons:

1. It's **not right** for you.

2. The **timing** is not right.

3. **Something better** is on the way.

Isn't that exciting? I believe in setbacks, or perhaps I shouldn't even call them setbacks. Let's call them plot twists. I believe plot twists are a gift from the universe to divert us onto the right path. They allow us to build resilience and grow when we are knocked down and move in the direction of bigger and better things. Whether we can see it now or not, the universe is always working in our favour. It is always steering us in the right direction. We must trust in its guidance.

PRIORITIES

Priorities. We all have them. We all live by them. They are present in every decision we make, every action we perform and every word we speak. However, only some of us are conscious of them. From the age of 5 to 17, ballet consumed much of my time. Almost every night after school and on Saturday mornings, I was in the dance studio doing jetes from the corner and pirouettes on my tippy toes. It took up a great chunk of my life because I loved it. Therefore, it was a priority. Then, when I entered year 12, my last year of schooling, I ditched dancing. My desire for a high ATAR (final year grades) outweighed my desire to become a dancer. I spent almost every night after school and Saturday mornings studying instead. Of course, I was devastated to stop dancing. However, I recognised a career as a full-time dancer wasn't my dream and thus, I shifted my time, energy and focus elsewhere. Whether I defined it at the time or not, study became a higher priority to me than dancing. When we choose to spend time doing one task over another, it's because we believe the former task holds higher priority. When you spend time prepping for a work meeting instead of having dinner with your partner, or getting your hair done instead of going for a run, it's because you believe your work and appearance are higher priorities than your relationship and exercise. If this is really the case, we are never truly wasting time, as our priorities, or what we value the most, already dictate exactly how we spend our time. The issue is that many of us don't like what we prioritise. We often use the excuse of not having enough time to avoid confronting this. We think if only we could freeze the clock or add a few extra hours to the day. Hate to break it to you, but we can't. And even if we could, you'd probably fill up that time with the same priorities anyway.

To reassess our priorities, we must first take responsibility for our lives. We need to acknowledge that we are the sole architects of our days and how we choose to fill them. If you don't like what you do in your day-to-day, then it's time to accept and change that:

1. To begin, I recommend creating a list of everything you want to achieve within a specified time frame, be it the next day, week or month. Whatever feels most manageable for you. These items represent your priorities.

2. Now write a number next to each priority, one being the most important. This is the order in which you value each priority.

3. Lastly, set deadlines. There is nothing like a bit of time pressure to get the ball rolling. Next to each priority, write the exact date you want it accomplished by. The date should feel like a challenge, but still be within the realm of believability.

When I was 21, I decided it was time to get my driver's licence and I gave myself just over three months to get it before I turned 22. I wanted the independence and freedom that all my friends had of being able to hop in a car and scoot away. As I was already 21, I didn't need to build up any hours. I just needed to know how to drive, and more importantly, how to reverse parallel park without kissing the curb. As I made it a priority, I hired an instructor and booked weekly lessons. This took a chunk of time away from my work and social life, but because it was a priority, I was willing to accept that. I had my driver's licence within the next two months.

To elevate your commitment to a priority, you can also share your deadline with a close friend or relative. Their support can help to keep you accountable to that date. As shifting our priorities means shifting how we spend our time, it can be daunting to start. Any kind of change always is. What it boils down to is how badly you want it and what time sacrifices you're willing to make. If feasible, you might even consider hiring someone or delegating tasks to other people. Apparently, I have been living under a rock for the past few years because I just discovered Airtasker and it quite literally blew my mind. The concept is simple. You post a task online that you need help with, it locates someone in your area who can help, and they complete the task for a quick buck. Genius. You can spend time focusing on your priorities whilst the ol' fella down the road does the gardening for you.

Confronting our fears and reassessing our priorities will enable us to allocate our time to tasks that empower us and help us to grow. If you're aiming to prioritise your health but often find yourself opting for takeout instead of cooking, then the upcoming chapter is tailored to you. Contrary to belief, healthy plant-based cooking does not have to be time-consuming. With simple recipes like a 25-minute curry or a 15-minute pasta, you can whip up nutritious meals in the same amount of time it takes you to scroll through UberEATS and debate whether to order Thai or Italian food. You can also dedicate time to other tasks, such as those you've been putting off due to fear or that you have just decided to make a priority. All my quick dinner recipes require 35 minutes or less to cook, offering ease, flavour and even leftovers for the next day's enjoyment. So put down that phone, pick up that knife and get chopping.

golden butter bean stew.

SERVES 3 **PREP TIME** 10 MINUTES **COOK TIME** 20 MINUTES

This golden butter bean stew is packed with antioxidants, colour and flavour from the magical spice that is turmeric. I love dolloping some coconut yoghurt on top and drizzling over chilli oil for extra creaminess and spice.

STEW
1 tablespoon olive oil
½ brown onion, finely diced
1 clove garlic, finely chopped
1 tablespoon finely chopped ginger
1½ teaspoons ground turmeric
1 teaspoon ground cumin
½ teaspoon ground coriander
2 tablespoons tomato paste
400 g can full-fat coconut milk
1 cup (250 ml) vegetable stock
2 × 400 g cans butter beans, drained and rinsed
3 large handfuls baby spinach leaves
juice of 1 lime

TO SERVE
4 pieces flatbread of your choice

TO SERVE (OPTIONAL)
coconut yoghurt, chilli flakes and coriander leaves

1. To make the stew, heat the olive oil in a frying pan over medium heat. Add the onion and sauté for 3–4 minutes, or until translucent.
2. Add the garlic, ginger, turmeric, cumin and coriander and sauté for another 30–60 seconds, or until fragrant.
3. Stir in the tomato paste, coconut milk, vegetable stock and butter beans. Mix well and bring to the boil, then reduce heat to medium-low. Simmer for 10–12 minutes, or until thickened.
4. Add the spinach and season well with salt and pepper. Cook for a further 2 minutes, stirring regularly, or until the spinach has wilted. Add the lime juice and stir through.
5. Serve with flatbread on the side, and top with coconut yoghurt, chilli flakes and coriander if you like.

TIP

This stew is also delicious on top of quinoa, rice or even roasted potatoes.

I am fully present in each moment, putting love and energy into every second.

the best (ever) vegan nachos.

SERVES 5   **PREP TIME** 25 MINUTES   **COOK TIME** 10 MINUTES

Everyone has a good nachos recipe, so here is mine. Except this one is not just good, it's great. With layers of chilli beans, guacamole, pico de gallo and a creamy cashew queso, it truly has all the best toppings.

GUACAMOLE
2 large avocados
juice of 1 lime
½ teaspoon ground cumin

PICO DE GALLO
2 tomatoes, finely diced
½ small red onion, finely diced
1 jalapeño pepper, seeded and finely diced
juice of 1 lime
⅓ cup coriander leaves, chopped

CHILLI BEANS
1 tablespoon olive oil
½ small red onion, finely diced
1 clove garlic, finely chopped
1 teaspoon chilli powder
1 teaspoon ground cumin
½ teaspoon ground coriander
¼ cup (70 g) tomato paste
1 tablespoon rice malt syrup
2 × 400 g cans black beans, drained and rinsed

TO ASSEMBLE
500 g bag corn chips
1 quantity cashew queso (page 56)
1 quantity pickled onions (page 94)
¼ cup coriander leaves
1 jalapeño, seeded and diced
3 limes, cut into wedges

1. Preheat oven to 180°C.
2. For the guacamole, scoop the avocado flesh into a bowl and add the lime juice, cumin and a pinch of salt and pepper. Mash until almost smooth.
3. To make the pico de gallo, mix all the ingredients in a bowl with a pinch of salt and pepper.
4. For the chilli beans, heat the olive oil in a frying pan over medium heat. Add the onion and sauté for 2–3 minutes, until translucent. Add the garlic, chilli powder, cumin, coriander and a pinch of salt and pepper. Cook for a further 30 seconds or until fragrant. Add the tomato paste, rice malt syrup and black beans and cook for 3–4 minutes, stirring regularly, or until the sauce has thickened slightly. Remove from heat.
5. Meanwhile, spread the corn chips evenly over two large baking trays and bake for 5 minutes, switching the bottom and top trays halfway, until heated.
6. To assemble the nachos, drizzle half the queso over the corn chips on one tray. Top with half the chilli beans, half the guacamole and half the pico de gallo. Add the other half of corn chips on top, drizzle with the remaining queso and spoon on the remaining chilli beans, guacamole and pico de gallo. Garnish with pickled onion, coriander and jalapeños. Serve with lime wedges to squeeze over.

Each time I face my fears, I become stronger and more resilient.

creamy green pasta.

SERVES 4   **PREP TIME** 10 MINUTES   **COOK TIME** 15 MINUTES

This pasta is a mix between a creamy vegan alfredo and pesto. The cashews and nutritional yeast give it a gloriously cheesy flavour, whilst the spinach and peas add a good serving of vegetables.

GREEN SAUCE
1 cup (150 g) raw cashews
1 cup (120 g) frozen peas
2 large handfuls baby spinach leaves
1 cup basil leaves
½ cup flat-leaf parsley leaves
½ cup (30 g) nutritional yeast
1 tablespoon tahini
juice of ½ lemon
1 clove garlic
1¼ cup (310 ml) soy milk

PASTA
500 g pasta (of your choice)

TO SERVE (OPTIONAL)
vegan parmesan, chilli flakes and olive oil

1. Soak the cashews in boiling water for 10 minutes, then drain. Heat a frying pan over medium heat and add the frozen peas. Cook for 3 minutes, stirring constantly, or until thawed. Add the spinach and cook for a further 2 minutes, or until wilted. Remove from heat.

2. Combine the peas and spinach, basil, parsley, cashews, nutritional yeast, tahini, lemon juice, garlic, soy milk and a pinch of salt and pepper in a blender. Blend until smooth. The consistency should be thick but pourable. Add more soy milk if needed.

3. Meanwhile, bring a large saucepan of water to the boil. Add the pasta and cook according to package instructions until al dente. Drain the pasta and transfer back into the pot.

4. Pour the sauce over the pasta. Mix well and cook for a minute or so to heat through. Transfer to serving bowls. If you like, top with vegan parmesan and chilli flakes and a drizzle of olive oil.

TIP

Opting for a gluten-free bean pasta, such as those made from chickpea or lentil flour, is a great way to bump up the protein of this dish.

Each moment holds infinite potential, and I seize the opportunity to create positive change in my life.

carrot noodle soup.

GFO **RSF**

SERVES 4 **PREP TIME** 10 MINUTES **COOK TIME** 25 MINUTES

If you follow me online then you might be thinking, isn't carrot noodle soup one of your popular budget recipes? Yes, you are correct. However, as it has more ingredients than the six-ingredient rule in the previous chapter, I've popped it into quick dinners. It'll take you just 35 minutes, is budget-friendly and will become one of your new go-to recipes!

5 large carrots (325 g), chopped into roughly 2 cm chunks
100 g rice vermicelli noodles
2 cups (500 ml) vegetable stock
400 ml can full-fat coconut milk
1 tablespoon olive oil
½ brown onion, finely diced
1 clove garlic, finely chopped
2½ tablespoons vegan Thai red curry paste
400 g can chickpeas, drained and rinsed

TO SERVE
4 slices bread of your choice, toasted

TO SERVE (OPTIONAL)
coconut yoghurt, coriander leaves, chilli oil and crushed peanuts

1. Place the carrots into a saucepan and fill with enough water to cover. Bring to the boil over high heat. Reduce the heat to medium and simmer for 15 minutes or until the carrots are tender. Remove from heat and drain.

2. Meanwhile, place the rice vermicelli noodles into a large heatproof bowl. Cover with boiling water and soak for 3 minutes. Drain and set aside.

3. Combine the carrots, vegetable stock, coconut milk, and a pinch of salt and pepper in a high-speed blender. Blend until smooth.

4. Heat the olive oil in a frying pan over medium heat. Add the onion and sauté for 3–4 minutes, until translucent. Add the garlic, red curry paste and chickpeas and sauté for a further 1–2 minutes, until fragrant.

5. Pour in the carrot mixture and vermicelli noodles and mix well. Reduce heat to medium-low and cook for 7–10 minutes, stirring regularly, or until the soup has thickened. Remove from heat.

6. To serve, ladle into bowls and serve with the toast. If you like, top with coconut yoghurt, coriander, chilli oil and crushed peanuts.

TIP

Feel free to substitute the chickpeas with any type of bean or legume. Diced tofu is also a delicious addition.

I am in control of how I use my time, and I choose to invest it in activities that bring me joy and fulfilment.

 quick dinners.

gochujang tofu burger.

SERVES 5   **PREP TIME** 20 MINUTES   **COOK TIME** 4 MINUTES

This is the kind of burger you'll want to tuck into on a Friday night with a few friends over and good tunes playing in the background. The star of the show is the gochujang sauce, which is creamy, hot and full of flavour. To make it speedy, the burger 'patty' is grilled peanut tofu, which is paired with a shaved cucumber salad.

GOCHUJANG SAUCE
1¼ cups (190 g) raw cashews
juice of ½ lime
2½ gochujang (Korean chilli paste)
2 tablespoons tamari
2 tablespoons rice malt syrup
1 tablespoon toasted sesame oil
1 clove garlic
2.5 cm knob ginger, peeled, roughly chopped
½ teaspoon chilli powder

CUCUMBER SALAD
2 Lebanese cucumbers, shaved into ribbons
1 large carrot, shaved into ribbons
¼ cup coriander leaves, roughly chopped
1 teaspoon sesame seeds
juice of ½ lime
1 teaspoon toasted sesame oil

TOFU
1½ tablespoons peanut butter
1 tablespoon tamari
2 teaspoons lime juice
¼ teaspoon vegan curry powder
500 g extra-firm tofu, pressed and sliced into 5 rectangles

TO SERVE
5 ciabatta burger rolls or buns of your choice
3 avocados, sliced
¼ cup coriander leaves

1. To make the gochujang sauce, soak cashews in boiling water for 10 minutes then drain. Combine in a food processor with the remaining ingredients, ¾ cup (180 ml) water and a pinch of salt and pepper. Process until smooth and set aside in the fridge.

2. For the cucumber salad, place the cucumber, carrot, coriander and sesame seeds into a bowl. Drizzle over the lime juice and sesame oil and toss to coat. Set aside in the fridge.

3. To cook the tofu, mix the peanut butter, tamari, lime juice and curry powder in a small bowl. Lay out the tofu on a plate and brush both sides with the peanut marinade.

4. Heat an electric grill or ridged sandwich press. Place the tofu on the grill, close the lid and cook for 3–4 minutes, or until heated and imprinted with golden grill marks. Remove from heat.

5. To assemble the burgers, smother a dollop of the gochujang sauce on the base of each roll. Top with the cucumber salad, tofu, another dollop of the sauce, avocado and coriander. Close with the top of the burger bun.

TIP

If you love spice, I recommend adding an extra ½–1 tsp of chilli powder into the gochujang sauce.

I align my actions with my priorities, ensuring that I invest my time and energy into what truly matters to me.

eggy nasi goreng.

SERVES 4 **PREP TIME** 15 MINUTES **COOK TIME** 20 MINUTES

When I think about all the food I ate on my 2023 trip to Bali, one dish stands out. That dish is nasi goreng. It's smoky, tangy and full of flavour. This recipe is inspired by all the nasi goreng I devoured in Bali, only it's lighter, healthier and quicker to make.

NASI GORENG
1 cup (200 g) medium-grain rice
1 tablespoon toasted sesame oil
1 shallot, finely chopped
1 clove garlic, finely chopped
1 tablespoon finely chopped ginger
2 carrots, finely diced
1 capsicum, finely diced
¾ cup (90 g) frozen peas, thawed
¼ cup (60 ml) tamari
1 tablespoon rice malt syrup

SCRAMBLED TOFU 'EGGS'
1 tablespoon olive oil
1 shallot, finely chopped
1 clove garlic, finely chopped
375 g extra-firm tofu, pressed and crumbled into small chunks
¼ cup (60 ml) soy milk
2 tablespoon nutritional yeast
¼ teaspoon ground turmeric
¼ teaspoon smoked paprika

TO SERVE (OPTIONAL)
sesame seeds, chopped spring onions and lime wedges

1. For the nasi goreng, cook the rice in a large saucepan of boiling water for 12 minutes or until tender. Drain and set aside.

2. Meanwhile, to cook the scrambled tofu, heat the olive oil in a frying pan over medium heat. Add the shallot and sauté for 2–3 minutes or until translucent. Add the garlic and sauté for a further 30 seconds. Add the crumbled tofu, soy milk, nutritional yeast, turmeric, smoked paprika and a pinch of salt and pepper. Cook for 2–3 minutes, stirring constantly, until heated through and well combined. Transfer to a bowl.

3. To finish the nasi goreng, heat the sesame oil in the same frying pan over medium heat. Add the shallot and sauté for 2–3 minutes or until translucent. Add the garlic, ginger, carrots and capsicum and cook for about 8 minutes, stirring occasionally, or until the vegetables are tender.

4. Add the peas, tamari, rice malt syrup and a pinch of salt and pepper. Mix well and cook for a further 1–2 minutes, to heat through. Stir in the rice and scrambled tofu.

5. Divide between bowls. If you like, top with sesame seeds, coriander and spring onions and serve with a wedge of lime.

TIP

For a more traditional flavour, you can substitute the tamari and rice malt syrup with ¼ cup (60 ml) kecap manis.

I celebrate my victories over procrastination, knowing that each small step forward brings me closer to my dreams.

 quick dinners.

marry me gnocchi.

SERVES 4   **PREP TIME** 10 MINUTES   **COOK TIME** 12 MINUTES

This is my take on the viral 'Marry Me Chicken'. Only this one is plant-based, healthier and quicker to make than its viral counterpart. Plus, who doesn't love the chewy and carby goodness that is gnocchi?

MARRY ME SAUCE
1 tbsp olive oil
½ brown onion, finely diced
1 clove garlic, finely chopped
¼ cup (15 g) nutritional yeast
2 teaspoons dried Italian herbs
1 teaspoon chilli flakes
1 cup (250 ml) vegetable stock
270 ml can full-fat coconut cream
400 g can diced tomatoes
½ cup (75 g) drained sun-dried tomatoes, chopped
¼ cup (70 g) tomato paste

GNOCCHI
500 g gnocchi

TO SERVE (OPTIONAL)
coconut yoghurt, basil leaves and chilli flakes

1. To make the sauce, heat the olive oil in a frying pan over medium heat. Add the onion and sauté for 3–4 minutes, or until translucent. Add the garlic, nutritional yeast, Italian herbs and chilli flakes and cook for 30–60 seconds or until fragrant.

2. Add the vegetable stock, coconut cream, diced tomatoes, sun-dried tomatoes, tomato paste and a pinch of salt and pepper. Cook for 5–7 minutes, or until thickened.

3. Meanwhile, bring a large saucepan of water to the boil over high heat. Add the gnocchi and cook for 3–4 minutes, or until the gnocchi floats to the top. Use a slotted spoon to transfer the gnocchi to the sauce and gently stir to coat.

4. Divide the gnocchi and sauce among bowls. If you like, top with coconut yoghurt, basil leaves and chilli flakes.

TIP

You can swap out the gnocchi for any pasta of your choice, including gluten-free pasta.

I am mindful of how I allocate my time and resources, ensuring that they support my priorities.

thai green curry.

GF **RSF**

SERVES 3   **PREP TIME** 10 MINUTES   **COOK TIME** 22 MINUTES

There is nothing quite like a hot and hearty bowl of Thai green curry that gives you a little sweat while you eat it. This is my delicious cheat's version as it only takes 22 minutes to bubble on the stovetop and is packed full of nutrients.

GREEN CURRY BASE
1 tablespoon olive oil
1 shallot, chopped
2 carrots, diced
1 clove garlic, finely chopped
1 tablespoon fresh ginger, finely diced
2 tablespoons vegan Thai green curry paste
400 g can full-fat coconut milk
1½ cups (375 ml) vegetable stock
1 tablespoon rice malt syrup
1 stalk lemongrass, bruised
juice of ½ lime
8 asparagus spears, ends trimmed
1 handful (roughly 80 g) green beans, ends trimmed
½ cup (60 g) frozen peas

TO SERVE
1 cup (200 g) Jasmine rice
2 teaspoons toasted sesame oil
350 g extra-firm tofu, pressed and diced

TO SERVE (OPTIONAL)
sliced red chilli, coriander leaves and lime wedges

1. For the serving ingredients, cook the rice in a large saucepan of boiling water for 12 minutes or until tender. Drain and keep warm.

2. Meanwhile, heat the sesame oil in a frying pan over medium heat. Add the tofu and cook for 3 minutes, flipping regularly, or until golden. Remove from heat and transfer to a bowl.

3. To make the green curry base, heat the oil in a large saucepan over medium heat. Add the shallot and carrots. Sauté for 1–2 minutes or until the shallot is translucent. Add the garlic, ginger and green curry paste and sauté for a further 30–60 seconds or until fragrant.

4. Add the coconut milk, vegetable stock, rice malt syrup, lemongrass and lime juice. Bring to the boil, reduce the heat slightly and simmer for 7 minutes.

5. Remove the lemongrass stalk and add the asparagus, green beans and peas. Cook for 7 minutes or until the vegetables are tender. Add the tofu and cook for a further minute to heat through.

6. To serve, spoon the rice into serving bowls and top with the curry. If you like, top with sliced chilli and coriander leaves, and serve with lime wedges.

TIP

Feel free to add any vegetables you like to this curry. For example, if you want to use up the old zucchini in the back of your fridge instead of buying new asparagus, go ahead!

I acknowledge my fears, but I do not let them control me.

rainbow peanut noodles.

SERVES 5 **PREP TIME** 15 MINUTES **COOK TIME** 20 MINUTES

The only thing better than a pot of gold at the end of a rainbow is a pot of these peanut noodles. Featuring my go-to creamy peanut sauce, soba noodles and a mix of colourful veggies and legumes. This is a big call from mum, but it is her favourite recipe. So, take her word for it and give it a go!

TAMARI TOFU
500 g extra-firm tofu, pressed and diced into cubes
1½ tablespoons tamari
1 tablespoon vegan fish sauce
2 teaspoons toasted sesame oil
1 tablespoon sesame seeds

PEANUT SAUCE
½ cup (140 g) peanut butter
juice of 1 lime
2 tablespoons tamari
1 tablespoon rice malt syrup
2 teaspoons vegan yellow curry paste
2 teaspoons finely chopped ginger

STIR-FRY
2 teaspoons toasted sesame oil
1 shallot, finely chopped
1 clove garlic, finely chopped
1 bunch broccolini, ends trimmed, each stem halved lengthways
1 zucchini, cut lengthways and diced into quarters
1 capsicum, sliced into thin strips
1 cup (165 g) edamame beans, shelled and cooked
2 heads pak choy, chopped

TO SERVE
270 g soba noodles

TO SERVE (OPTIONAL)
chopped spring onion, coriander leaves, sesame seeds, crushed peanuts and lime wedges

1. For the tamari tofu, place the tofu into a large bowl. Drizzle over the tamari, vegan fish sauce and sesame oil and toss to coat. Cover and marinate in the fridge until needed.

2. To make the peanut sauce, place all the ingredients, ¼ cup (60 ml) water and a pinch of pepper in a small bowl and mix well. Add a dash more water if too thick. Set aside.

3. To cook tofu, heat a frying pan over medium heat. Add tofu pieces, reserving excess marinade, and cook for 5 minutes, flipping regularly, until golden. Pour in the reserved marinade and sesame seeds and allow to sizzle for 30–40 seconds. Remove from heat and cover with foil to keep warm.

4. For the stir-fry, heat the sesame oil in a large frying pan over medium heat. Add the shallot and sauté for 2–3 minutes or until translucent. Add the garlic and broccolini and sauté for a further 2–3 minutes until broccolini is just starting to soften.

5. Add the zucchini and capsicum and cook for 3 minutes, stirring regularly. Add the edamame beans and pak choy and cook for 2 minutes, or until the pak choy has begun to wilt. Stir in the peanut sauce and cook for another minute to heat through. Remove from heat.

6. Meanwhile, cook the soba noodles in a large saucepan of boiling water for 4 minutes. Drain.

7. To serve, lay the soba noodles in the base of serving bowls. Top with the peanut stir-fry and tamari tofu. If you like, top with chopped spring onion, coriander leaves, sesame seeds and crushed peanuts, and serve with lime wedges.

I confront my fears head-on, knowing that doing so leads to personal growth and empowerment.

bbq mushroom flatbreads.

SERVES 4 **PREP TIME** 20 MINUTES **COOK TIME** 17 MINUTES (+ WARMING FLATBREADS IF DESIRED)

Mushrooms are one of, if not the, most interesting ingredients out there. There are thousands of edible varieties and so many ways to cook, texture and flavour them. For this recipe, we are going with Swiss browns, as they are quick to cook, and shiitake for their dense, fleshy fibres.

MISO BEAN MASH
2 × 400 g cans butter beans, drained and rinsed
¼ cup (70 g) tahini
juice of ½ lemon
1 clove garlic
1 tablespoon white miso paste
1 tablespoon tamari
¼ tsp smoked paprika
2 tablespoons soy milk

ROCKET SALAD
3 handfuls baby rocket
½ Lebanese cucumber, diced
¼ cup flat-leaf parsley leaves, roughly chopped
2 tablespoons mint leaves
juice of ½ lemon

BBQ MUSHROOMS
1 tablespoon olive oil
2 × 200 g punnets Swiss brown mushroom, sliced
2 × 100 g punnets shiitake mushroom, sliced
1 clove garlic, finely chopped
½ teaspoon smoked paprika
½ teaspoon chilli powder
¼ cup (70 g) tomato paste
2 tablespoons balsamic vinegar
1 tablespoon tamari
1 tablespoon rice malt syrup
2 teaspoons Dijon mustard

TO SERVE
4 large flatbreads (of your choice)
pickled onions (page 94), sesame seeds and lemon wedges

1. To make the miso bean mash, place all the ingredients into a food processor and add a pinch of salt and pepper. Process until smooth.

2. For the rocket salad, place the rocket, cucumber, parsley and mint leaves in a large bowl. Drizzle over the lemon juice and toss to combine.

3. For the BBQ mushrooms, heat a frying pan over medium heat. Add the mushrooms and cook for 3–5 minutes without stirring. Flip and cook for another 5 minutes, without stirring, or until the liquid has reduced and mushrooms are beginning to brown.

4. Add the olive oil, garlic, smoked paprika and chilli powder. Cook for 2 minutes, stirring continuously.

5. Add the tomato paste, balsamic vinegar, tamari, rice malt syrup, Dijon mustard and a pinch of salt and pepper and mix well. Cook for a further 5 minutes, stirring continuously, or until the sauce has thickened.

6. To serve, heat the flatbread in a frying pan over medium heat for 1–2 minutes. Place the flatbreads onto serving plates and dollop on the miso bean mash. Top with rocket salad and BBQ mushrooms. If you like, top with pickled onion and sesame seeds and serve with lemon wedges.

*I am not defined by my fears,
I am defined by my courage to overcome them.*

cheat's dhal.

SERVES 4   **PREP TIME** 10 MINUTES   **COOK TIME** 20 MINUTES

Dhal made the traditional way can take hours to slow cook, but this version is done in less than 30 minutes! It uses the ground spices of cumin, turmeric and cinnamon to pack a punch of flavour and pre-cooked canned lentils to speed up the process.

1 cup (200 g) basmati rice
1 tablespoon olive oil
½ brown onion, finely diced
2 cloves garlic, finely chopped
2 teaspoons finely chopped ginger
1 large bay leaf
1 tablespoon vegan curry powder
1 teaspoon ground cumin
½ teaspoon ground turmeric
¼ teaspoon ground cinnamon
2 tablespoons tomato paste
400 g can diced tomatoes
400 ml can full-fat coconut milk
⅓ cup (80 g) coconut yoghurt
2 x 400 g cans lentils, drained and rinsed

TO SERVE (OPTIONAL)
coconut yoghurt, coriander leaves and sliced red chilli

1. Cook the rice in a large saucepan of boiling water for 12 minutes or until tender. Drain and keep warm.

2. Meanwhile, heat the olive oil in a large saucepan over medium heat. Add the onion and sauté for 3–4 minutes or until translucent. Add the garlic and ginger and sauté for a further minute.

3. Add the bay leaf, curry powder, cumin, turmeric, cinnamon, and a pinch of salt and pepper and mix well. Cook, stirring constantly, for 20–30 seconds or until fragrant. Stir in the tomato paste and ½ cup (125 ml) water cook for 2–3 minutes, stirring regularly, or until a thick brown paste forms.

4. Add the diced tomatoes, coconut milk, coconut yoghurt and lentils. Bring to the boil. Reduce the heat to medium-low. Simmer for 10 minutes, stirring occasionally, or until the dhal has thickened.

5. To serve, spoon the dhal and rice into bowls. If you like, top with a dollop of coconut yoghurt, coriander leaves and red chilli.

TIP

This is also delicious served with some warm naan bread to soak up all the curry.

I am grateful for the time I have been given, and I cherish each moment as a precious gift.

nut-free mac and cheese.

GFO **RSF**

SERVES 4   **PREP TIME** 10 MINUTES   **COOK TIME** 15 MINUTES

This recipe goes out to my nut-allergy gang. You can still enjoy a cosy and comforting dairy-free mac and cheese without a nut in sight.

400 g macaroni or your choice of pasta
150 g extra-firm tofu
4 cups (1 litre) soy milk
½ cup (30 g) nutritional yeast
2 teaspoons Dijon mustard
1 teaspoon garlic powder
1 teaspoon onion powder
½ teaspoon smoked paprika
¼ teaspoon ground turmeric
¼ cup (60 ml) olive oil
⅓ cup (50 g) plain flour

TO SERVE (OPTIONAL)
toasted breadcrumbs and smoked paprika

1. Cook the macaroni in a large saucepan of boiling water according to package instructions until al dente. Drain and set aside.

2. Place the tofu, soy milk, nutritional yeast, Dijon mustard, garlic powder, onion powder, smoked paprika, turmeric and a pinch of salt and pepper into a food processor. Process until smooth. Set aside.

3. Heat the olive oil in a saucepan over medium-high heat. Add the flour and whisk for 1–2 minutes, until evenly combined.

4. Pour in the 'cheese' sauce while briskly whisking. Continue whisking for 2–4 minutes until the sauce has thickened.

5. Mix in the macaroni and remove from heat. Divide among bowls and if you like, top with breadcrumbs and smoked paprika.

TIPS

For a gluten-free option, use a gluten-free plain flour and gluten-free pasta such as red lentil or chickpea pasta.

I am empowered to make conscious choices about how I spend my time, ensuring that they align with my values and goals.

brothy coconut noodles.

SERVES 4 **PREP TIME** 15 MINUTES **COOK TIME** 20 MINUTES

You just can't beat noodles in soup, so here's another noodle soup recipe for you. This easy and flavourful turmeric and coconut broth-style soup will take you under 30 minutes yet packs so much colour and spice. Serve with a wedge of lime, fresh herbs and chilli oil for extra flavour.

BROTH
2 shallots, roughly chopped
2 cloves garlic, roughly chopped
7.5 cm knob ginger, peeled and roughly chopped
1 heaped tablespoon finely chopped lemongrass
finely grated zest and juice of ½ lime
1 tablespoon olive oil
2 teaspoons ground turmeric
1 tablespoon rice malt syrup
1 tablespoon white miso paste
3 cups (750 ml) vegetable stock
400 ml can full-fat coconut milk

NOODLES
450 g extra-firm tofu, pressed and diced
150 g rice vermicelli noodles

PAK CHOY
1 tablespoon olive oil
1 clove garlic
1 teaspoon finely chopped ginger
4 heads pak choy, halved lengthwise

TO SERVE (OPTIONAL)
coriander leaves, chilli oil, sesame seeds and lime wedges

1. For the broth, place the shallots, garlic, ginger, lemongrass and lime zest into a small food processor and process to a smooth paste.

2. Heat the olive oil in a saucepan over medium heat. Add the paste and sauté for 2–3 minutes or until fragrant. Stir in the turmeric and a pinch of salt and pepper and cook for 1 more minute.

3. Add the rice malt syrup, miso paste, vegetable stock, coconut milk, lime juice and ½ cup (125ml) water and mix well. Bring to the boil then reduce heat to low. Add the diced tofu and simmer for 7–8 minutes, partially covered, stirring occasionally.

4. Meanwhile, place the vermicelli noodles into a large heatproof bowl. Cover with boiling water and soak for 5 minutes. Drain and set aside.

5. For the pak choy, heat the olive oil in a deep-frying pan or wok over medium heat. Add the garlic and ginger and sauté for 30–60 seconds. Add the pak choy and a pinch of salt and pepper and cook for 2 minutes, using tongs to flip regularly. Add 2 tablespoons water, cover and cook for 2 more minutes. Remove from heat.

6. To serve, place vermicelli noodles into bowls and pour over the broth. Spoon in the tofu. Place the pak choy on top. If you like, top with coriander leaves, chilli oil and sesame seeds, and serve with a wedge of lime.

I have supportive and trustworthy friends who I can rely on to keep me accountable to my priorities.

cauliflower floret focaccia sandwich.

SERVES 3   **PREP TIME** 15 MINUTES   **COOK TIME** 25 MINUTES

Who said you can't have a sandwich for dinner? This focaccia sandwich is packed with tender and smoky roasted cauliflower and smothered in a quick, high-protein Romesco sauce. It packs a punch of flavour, protein, fibre and nutrients.

ROMESCO SAUCE
3 roasted red capsicums from a jar, drained, about 1½ cups (330 g)
400 g can diced tomatoes
1 clove garlic
200 g extra-firm tofu
1 cup (160 g) blanched almonds
¼ cup flat-leaf parsley leaves
¼ cup (15 g) nutritional yeast
2 tablespoons olive oil
2 tablespoons soy milk
juice of ½ lemon

CAULIFLOWER FLORETS
1 large head cauliflower, chopped into small florets
¼ cup (30 g) rice breadcrumbs
1 tablespoon olive oil

TO SERVE
3 focaccia bread rolls, sliced in half
3 cups baby rocket
¼ cup (60 g) crumbled vegan feta

1. Preheat the oven to 220°C and line a baking tray with baking paper.
2. To make the Romesco sauce, place the capsicum, diced tomatoes, garlic, tofu, almonds, parsley, nutritional yeast, olive oil, soy milk, lemon juice and a pinch of salt and pepper into a food processor. Process until smooth.
3. Put the cauliflower florets into a large mixing bowl and add ¾ cup (180 ml) of the Romanesco sauce, the rice breadcrumbs and olive oil. Toss until the florets are well coated.
4. Spread the cauliflower over the baking tray and bake for 25 minutes, turning halfway, or until fork tender and browning around the edges.
5. To serve, smother the bottom half of the focaccia with some Romesco sauce. Top with the cauliflower florets, rocket and vegan feta. Close with the top half of the focaccia.

TIP

For a gluten-free option, you can use two thick slices of gluten-free bread to replace the focaccia.

Time is always on my side.

no-bake desserts.

take the 'no-bake' path.

Growing up, I wished I was one of those kids who knew exactly what they wanted to be when they were older. A pilot, one would say. A nurse the next. And me? I just wanted to be Chloe. Which was both confusing and liberating at the same time. I had no game plan; all I knew was that I wanted to be successful at what I did. When I graduated from high school with good grades, I thought it must mean that university was the path for me. With the added pressure of friends, family and teachers, I enrolled. I applied for biomedicine and commerce at the University of Melbourne, got accepted into both and chose to go with commerce. Two weeks in and I already hated it. I got a terrible flu, I got lost on campus an embarrassing number of times and to top it off, I got hit on the head by a boom gate. How I managed to stand and pause beneath the gates of a boom gate without realising it still baffles me to this day. But all I remember is feeling a big whack on my noggin, falling to the ground, and hearing a bunch of older students walk past me laughing and muttering 'Stupid freshie'. Which, in all honesty, hurt more than the swollen bump on my head. If that wasn't enough of a sign from the universe to leave, I don't know what was. So, I dropped out and thank gosh I did.

Knowing what to do with our lives can be confusing at any age. With everyone telling us what we should and shouldn't be, it can be difficult to navigate where to go. From a young age, we are told what not to do. Heck, some of the first words we learn are no and don't. No, don't eat that. No, don't touch that. And when we are older it's, no, don't think that, feel that or be that. Rarely are we told, yes, go ahead, do that. Consequently, many of us fall into the trap of doing what our family, friends and society deem as right, in jobs that we hate, and only doing the things that we love on the weekend. If I asked you to close your eyes and visualise exactly what your dream career looked like, what would you be doing? What is it that you do on the weekend to fill your cup? What are you truly passionate about? Perhaps you love sitting on the couch and watching movies. Can't say that I don't love a good horror movie and popcorn session myself. Did you know that many streaming platforms hire people to watch and rate their TV shows and movies before they're released? Yep. Someone is watching the next season of your favourite show right now and getting paid for it. Or maybe you just like to sleep. Who doesn't? Did you know that a Finnish hotel employs a full-time sleeper to critique the comfort of their beds? This means that there are people out there literally getting paid to sleep! I'm jealouzzzzz. Believe me when I say that there is opportunity in every field. The first step is just about getting clear on what you love doing. For me, you're reading it!

If you don't know where your passions lie yet, that's great too. I suggest writing a list of all the things that excite you; painting, reading, running, cooking or whatever it might be. Then, once you've written a list, circle the three that make you smile the most. Boom, you've discovered your top three passions. Now, begin searching online for jobs in those fields. Some might require further study, and some might simply require you to submit a resume. I truly believe that what we are meant to do on this planet will unfold organically if we allow it, no matter how unorthodox or 'no-bake' that path might look. If you are currently working in a job that drains you physically and mentally, it is going to suck you dry of any energy that you could be putting towards where your passions lie. As soon as you get on the thought pattern of 'what if' and discover the endless career opportunities that lie before you, the universe will follow suit and guide you in the right direction. If you had told me a few years ago that I'd be a full-time content creator, filming and sharing recipes with millions of people all over the world, I would have laughed at you. I might have even checked your temperature or offered to pour you a drink (just herbal tea, of course). But what I didn't realise is that the universe was already guiding me there, step by step, until suddenly, I had my first brand deal signed within a week of leaving my previous job. Was it small? Yes. $90 for seven hours of work small. But it was a start. If finances are a barrier for you, you could try cutting down the hours at your current job bit by bit. Allowing yourself more time to dedicate towards your passions until slowly but surely they become your full-time job. If, like me, you find affirmations particularly helpful, here are some that I recommend repeating and writing down in your journal daily as discussed in Chapter 1:

- 'I am worthy of my dream job.'
- 'I feel supported and guided by the universe.'
- 'I love working as a (your dream job) because (why you'd love it).'
- 'I have the freedom to work in a job that I love.'

It's one thing to be clear on your career direction but moving through your limiting beliefs to get there is a whole other ball game. Although I touched on fear in an earlier chapter, I wanted to touch on it again here. In particular, the fear of judgement when chasing your 'no-bake' career goals. When I first opened a food-focused Instagram account to pursue content creation, I was so embarrassed that everyone, especially my friends, would find out. So, to avoid any embarrassment, I blocked my whole school year level. I wish I were joking. I spent hours typing up everyone's Instagram handles and blocking them one by one. Then a few months later when I had grown to a following of 1000 people, a girl from the year level below me followed the account. I gasped. The shock of seeing her name pop up could have sent me into a coma. I didn't even consider the need to block the year level below me and I was punching myself for it. To make matters worse, she was friends with a few of my close friends. I was one conversation away from being exposed. So, I did what any sane person would do. I moved countries and changed my name. I'm kidding, even though I felt like it at the time. When I walked past the girl at school the next day, we caught each other's gaze. I knew that she knew that I knew she followed me, and I bet she wondered why no one else from our school did. So, on top of my worry about people finding out about my account was now the worry that people would find out they had been blocked by my account. That night I spent hours unblocking everyone and shortly after told my friends about the whole thing. Want to know their reaction? They hugged and congratulated me for the account. All that worrying about what my friends would think was for nothing. Don't get me wrong, there were still giggles and gossip behind my back from people who weren't in my inner circle. And yeah, that sucked. But what would have sucked even more is letting that stop me doing what I loved doing. I mean, look at where persisting with that Instagram account has got me today. Writing my very first cookbook that you are reading right now. OMG! I couldn't be more grateful.

My biggest piece of advice to to help you move through the fear of judgement would be to know that someone is always going to judge you. I know that doesn't sound very comforting but let me explain. It doesn't matter if you take up dance classes, drop out of university or post yourself making a no-bake dessert online, there is always going to be someone who judges you. The good thing is that why they judge you has nothing to do with you and all to do with them. For me, it's usually good ol' @user_1234 leaving a spicy hate comment because they don't believe that I can call my recipe healthy if it contains oats. For the love of god, leave oats alone. However, if it's your family, friends or pets judging you, because we all know that cats can give the biggest side-eye, you've got to ask yourself this. If they were in your position, would they do the same thing? Would they take that inspired action, follow that dream or chase that career if the opportunity presented itself? The most likely answer is yes. Because, in a sense, we are all selfish beings. We always do what we feel is best for us. Even if we think we are doing something for someone else, we are still doing it for ourselves. It's like saying the only reason you work for your family's business is because you think it'll appease your father. In that case, appeasing your father was your goal and you chose to work for the family business to achieve that. Your dad is not to blame, you are. If the people closest to you are the ones judging you and aren't supportive of your career, then perhaps it's better to accept them for who they are and set boundaries within those relationships. For example, I have many friends who aren't vegan. Just because we don't share that same value, doesn't mean we can't be friends and share similar values elsewhere. It just means that it is an area we don't discuss in detail with each other. They know my standpoint on it, and I know theirs, and we appreciate, love and support each other anyway. So, to summarise, stop worrying about judgement. You can't stop it, so you might as well do what you want to do anyway.

Imposter syndrome is another challenge many of us will face as we move into a new career. If you were to read through the Word documents on my computer from the past five years, you'd see at least 10 half-written books. That's the equivalent of two books scrapped per year. I'd get stuck on one chapter or one recipe and give up on the whole thing entirely. This was caused by imposter syndrome. It's that icky feeling you get in the pit of your stomach when you feel incompetent or unqualified for a task, position or project. Every little mistake in my book was a constant reminder that one, I don't have any qualifications in the food space, and two, I don't have any qualifications in the writing space. Who in their right mind would want to make my recipes or read what I've got to say? Well, according to Instagram, apparently over a million of you. Imagine all the people I could have helped five years earlier if I had just released the need to be 'qualified' and instead focused on thinking, feeling and believing that I was good enough already. Because I am. And you are too.

So, I ask you, do you dare to be the no-bake carrot cake in a world of baked carrot cakes? For context, when I moved house, the oven in my new place was faulty. I had bought all the ingredients to film a carrot cake recipe, only to find that my oven wouldn't turn on. But everything happens for a reason, right? After a five-minute meltdown, an idea popped into my head. Why don't I attempt a no-bake version? I wasn't sure if it would work, but I persisted anyway. Long story short, the cake was incredible, and it racked up a whopping eight million views on Instagram. The universe is always guiding us in the right direction. It wants us to work and thrive in our dream career so that we can get more out of life and help others to do the same. A career that is in alignment with our authentic self will allow us to create positive change in the world, no matter how big or small that change is. Even if it's simply by encouraging one person to turn off the oven and shove their cake in the freezer instead. Let each recipe in this no-bake dessert chapter be a reminder that we can have our dream career, no matter how 'no-bake' it looks.

no-bake carrot cake.

SERVES 9 **PREP TIME** 20 MINUTES **SET TIME** 2 HOURS

Yes, this is the carrot cake. The one that racked up over eight million views despite me having a minor breakdown pre-filming. And, dare I say, this might be my favourite no-bake creation to date!

CARROT CAKE
1 cup (150 g) Medjool dates, pitted
2 carrots (130 g), grated
1 cup (90 g) rolled oats
1 cup desiccated coconut
1 cup (160 g) roasted almonds
2 teaspoons ground cinnamon
¼ teaspoon ground nutmeg
¼ teaspoon ground ginger
1 teaspoon vanilla extract
1 tablespoon oat milk

FROSTING
1 cup (150 g) raw cashews
3 Medjool dates, pitted
1 tablespoon tahini
1 teaspoon vanilla extract
½ cup (125 ml) oat milk, plus extra if needed

GARNISH
2 tablespoons walnuts, crumbled
¼ carrot, shaved into ribbons

1. For the carrot cake, soak the dates in boiling water for 5 minutes, then drain. Combine the grated carrot, rolled oats, desiccated coconut, roasted almonds, cinnamon, nutmeg, ginger, vanilla extract, oat milk and a pinch of salt in a food processor. Process until thick and smooth.

2. Line a 20.5 cm square cake tin with baking paper. Spoon in the carrot mixture and smooth with the back of a spoon.

3. To make the frosting, soak the cashews and dates in boiling water. Take the dates out after 5 minutes and soak the cashews for a further 5 minutes. Drain. Combine the dates, cashews, tahini, vanilla extract and oat milk in the food processor. Process until smooth, adding a dash more oat milk if needed to thin.

4. Dollop the frosting over the carrot cake and spread it with the back of a spoon. Set in the freezer for 2 hours.

5. Garnish with the walnuts and carrot ribbons. Cut into squares and serve.

TIP

I recommend storing leftovers of this cake in the fridge so that it is a soft and fudgy consistency for eating straight away. However, if you won't finish it within 3–4 days, it's perfectly fine to store it in the freezer and remove it 20 minutes before eating.

I trust in divine timing, knowing that the perfect career opportunities will manifest for me at the right time and in the right way.

chickpea cookie dough.

SERVES 5 **PREP TIME** 10 MINUTES

We all know that I love beans, so why not have them in a dessert? This chickpea cookie dough is healthier, gluten-free and incredibly addictive. Rest assured; you cannot taste the chickpeas. They just give it an irresistibly fudgy consistency while also adding some plant protein.

½ cup (75 g) Medjool dates, pitted
400 g can chickpeas, drained and rinsed
⅓ cup (95 g) peanut butter
¼ cup (30 g) vanilla protein powder
¼ cup (60 ml) soy milk, plus extra if needed
¼ cup (60 ml) rice malt syrup
1 teaspoon vanilla extract
⅓ cup (65 g) dark chocolate chips

1. Soak the dates in boiling water for 5 minutes, then drain. Combine the chickpeas, peanut butter, vanilla protein powder, soy milk, rice malt syrup, vanilla extract, dates and a pinch of salt in a food processor.

2. Process until thick and smooth, stopping to scrape down the sides as needed. Add a dash more soy milk if too thick.

3. Transfer the mixture to a bowl and add the chocolate chips and mix well. Spoon mixture into jars and serve.

TIP

White beans also work well in this recipe if you don't have any chickpeas on hand.

I celebrate my uniqueness and honour the path that is uniquely mine.

no-bake desserts.

protein balls.

Protein balls are my go-to snack. These are my five favourite flavours that I rotate through weekly. Mocha, salted caramel and coconut, double chocolate chickpea, peanut butter cookie and raspberry ripe. All are sweet, perfectly chewy and great to have on hand for snacks. For the first four recipes, you'll need a high-speed blender or food processor to break the ingredients down into a chunky dough.

TIP

Protein balls can be stored in an air-tight container in the fridge for 4–5 days.

mocha protein balls.

MAKES 14   **PREP TIME** 20 MINUTES

1 cup (150 g) Medjool dates, pitted
1 cup (80 g) desiccated coconut
1 cup (100 g) walnuts
½ cup (60 g) vanilla protein powder
2 tablespoons freeze-dried instant coffee
2 tablespoons soy milk, plus more if needed
1 teaspoon vanilla extract
½ teaspoon ground cinnamon

FOR ROLLING
cacao or cocoa powder

1. Soak the dates in boiling water for 5 minutes, then drain. Combine the coconut, walnuts, vanilla protein powder, instant coffee, soy milk, vanilla extract, cinnamon, dates and a pinch of salt in a food processor.

2. Process until a thick dough forms, stopping to scrape down the sides as needed. Add a dash more soy milk if too dry. Scoop the dough into your hands and roll it into 14 balls.

3. Dust a layer of cacao or cocoa powder onto a plate. Roll the protein balls in it to coat.

salted caramel and coconut protein balls.

MAKES 12 **PREP TIME** 20 MINUTES

1 cup (150 g) Medjool dates, pitted
1 cup (150 g) unsalted roasted cashews
½ cup (60 g) vanilla protein powder
½ cup (40 g) desiccated coconut
1 teaspoon vanilla extract

FOR ROLLING
desiccated coconut

1. Soak the dates in boiling water for 5 minutes, then drain. Place the cashews into a food processor and process for about 10 minutes, stopping to scraping down the sides as needed, or until a smooth nut butter consistency forms.

2. Add the dates, vanilla protein powder, coconut, vanilla extract and a pinch of salt. Process until a thick dough forms, stopping to scrape down the sides as needed. Scoop the dough into your hands and roll it into 12 balls.

3. Sprinkle a layer of desiccated coconut onto a plate. Roll the protein balls in it to coat.

peanut butter cookie protein balls.

MAKES 18 **PREP TIME** 10 MINUTES

1 cup (90 g) rolled oats
⅓ cup (40 g) vanilla protein powder
2 tablespoons flaxseed meal
½ teaspoon ground cinnamon
1 cup (280 g) peanut butter
¼ cup (60 ml) rice malt syrup
1 teaspoon vanilla extract
¼ cup (60 ml) oat milk
¼ cup (45 g) dark chocolate chips or sultanas

1. Place the oats, protein powder, flaxseed meal, cinnamon and a pinch of salt into a food processor. Process until finely ground.

2. Add the peanut butter, rice malt syrup, vanilla extract and oat milk and process for a further 2 minutes, or until smooth.

3. Transfer the dough to a bowl and mix through the chocolate chips or sultanas. Scoop the dough into your hands and roll it into 18 balls.

no-bake desserts.

double chocolate chickpea balls.

MAKES 14   PREP TIME 30 MINUTES
SET TIME 10 MINUTES

1 cup (150 g) Medjool dates, pitted
400 g can chickpeas, drained and rinsed
⅓ cup (35 g) cacao powder
⅓ cup (40 g) vanilla protein powder
¼ cup (70 g) peanut butter
1 teaspoon vanilla extract
2 tablespoons oat milk

FOR COATING
80 g dark chocolate
1 tablespoon coconut oil

1. Soak the dates in boiling water for 5 minutes, then drain. Combine the chickpeas, cacao powder, vanilla protein powder, peanut butter, vanilla extract, oat milk, dates and a pinch of salt in a food processor.

2. Process until a thick dough forms, stopping to scrape down the sides as needed. Dampen your hands with water and scoop the dough into them. Roll it into 14 balls. Set aside in the fridge.

3. Place the chocolate and coconut oil into a small microwave-safe bowl. Microwave in 20-second increments, stirring between each, until fully melted. Alternatively, melt the chocolate and coconut oil on the stovetop in a double boiler.

4. Line a plate or tray with baking paper. Using a fork, dip each protein ball into the melted chocolate and turn until fully covered. Transfer to the lined plate and place in the fridge for 5–10 minutes, or until the chocolate has set.

I am creating a work life that inspires and excites me.

raspberry ripe protein balls.

MAKES 10   **PREP TIME** 20 MINUTES
SET TIME 55 MINUTES

2 cups (140 g) frozen raspberries
1 cup (80 g) desiccated coconut
⅓ cup (40 g) vanilla protein powder
1 tablespoon chia seeds
1 teaspoon vanilla extract

FOR COATING
80 g dark chocolate
1 tablespoon coconut oil
2 tablespoons freeze-dried raspberries, crushed

1. Place the frozen raspberries into a large bowl and stand for 10 minutes to thaw. Once softened, mash with a fork.

2. Add the desiccated coconut, protein powder, chia seeds, vanilla extract and a pinch of salt. Mash and mix until well combined.

3. Line a tray with baking paper. Scoop the mixture into your hands and roll it into 10 balls. Place onto the tray and set aside in the freezer for 40 minutes to firm up.

4. Place the chocolate and coconut oil into a small microwave-safe bowl. Microwave in 20-second increments, stirring between each, until fully melted. Alternatively, melt the chocolate and coconut oil on the stovetop in a double boiler.

5. Line a plate or tray with baking paper. Using a fork, dip each protein ball into the melted chocolate and turn until fully covered. Place onto the lined plate and quickly sprinkle over the freeze-dried raspberries before the chocolate sets. Refrigerate for 5–10 minutes, or until the chocolate has set.

New career opportunities always unfold organically for me.

no-bake desserts.

chocolate cherry tart.

SERVES 12 **PREP TIME** 20 MINUTES **SET TIME** 4 HOURS

Whether it's for Christmas lunch or a birthday dinner, if you want to bring something to the table that everyone is going to love, this chocolate cherry tart is it. It's easy, no-bake and the filling has only three ingredients. When everyone at the table asks you for the recipe because trust me, they will, be sure to send them to this cookbook!

BASE
2¼ cups (270 g) almond meal
⅓ cup (35 g) cacao powder
⅓ cup (60 g) coconut oil, melted
¼ cup (60 ml) rice malt syrup
1 teaspoon vanilla extract

FILLING
½ cup (125 ml) full-fat coconut milk
¼ cup (60 ml) cherry juice
220 g dark chocolate, chopped

TOPPING
¼ cup (40 g) fresh cherries, sliced in half and pitted
¼ cup (45 g) pomegranate seeds

1. Grease a 21 cm x 3.5 cm deep fluted tart tin with removable base.

2. To make the base, combine the almond meal, cacao powder and a pinch of salt in a large bowl. Mix well. Add the melted coconut oil, rice malt syrup and vanilla extract. Mix with your hands until a dough forms.

3. Gather the dough into a ball and transfer to the tart tin. Press out evenly to cover the base and sides. Refrigerate until needed.

4. For the filling, place the coconut milk and cherry juice into a saucepan. Bring to the boil over medium-high heat. Remove from heat and add the chocolate. Whisk until the chocolate is fully melted and smooth.

5. Pour the filling into the base. Top with the fresh cherry halves and pomegranate seeds. Refrigerate for 3–4 hours, until set. Cut into slices to serve.

TIP

When removing the tart from the tin, if it's stubborn, try going around the edge with a knife to loosen it.

I choose to live life on my own terms, unapologetically following my dream career without the fear of judgement.

nutty caramel slice.

SERVES 8 **PREP TIME** 20 MINUTES **SET TIME** 2 HOURS 10 MINUTES

I know you shouldn't read a book by its cover, but in the case of this slice, please, read ahead. It tastes just as good as it looks. It's no-bake, refined sugar-free and has three beautiful layers of almond, caramel and chocolate.

BASE
5 Medjool dates, pitted
1½ cups (240 g) roasted almonds
½ cup (40 g) desiccated coconut
2 tablespoon coconut oil

MIDDLE LAYER
1 cup (150 g) Medjool dates, pitted
⅓ cup (95 g) peanut butter
⅓ cup (80 ml) oat milk, plus more if needed
1 teaspoon vanilla extract

TOPPING
80 g dark chocolate
1 tablespoon coconut oil
sea salt flakes, to sprinkle

1. Line a container or loaf tin (about 24 cm × 13 cm × 6.5 cm) with baking paper, extending over the two long sides.

2. To make the base, soak the dates in boiling water for 5 minutes, then drain. Place the almonds, desiccated coconut, coconut oil and dates into a food processor. Process just until finely ground and the mixture is sticky. Be sure not to overprocess otherwise it will become an oily nut butter. Press the mixture over the base of the lined container.

3. For the middle layer, soak the dates in boiling water for 5 minutes, then drain. Place the peanut butter, oat milk, vanilla extract and dates into the cleaned food processor. Process into a smooth caramel. Add a dash more oat milk if needed to thin slightly. Dollop over the base layer and smooth with the back of a spoon. Pop in the freezer for 2 hours, until firm.

4. To make the topping, combine the chocolate and coconut oil in a small microwave-safe bowl. Microwave in 20-second increments, stirring between each, until fully melted. Alternatively, melt the chocolate and coconut oil on the stovetop in a double boiler.

5. Pour the chocolate over the slice and quickly spread with a spoon to coat evenly. Sprinkle with sea salt flakes and place in the fridge for 10 minutes, or until the chocolate has set. Use the paper to lift out of the container. Cut into slices to serve.

TIP

Store in the fridge for the perfect gooey caramel consistency. You can substitute any nut or seed butter you like for the peanut butter in the middle layer. Some of my other favourites are almond butter, cashew butter or tahini.

I find joy and fulfilment in my work, knowing that it aligns with my passions and purpose.

apple cream bark.

SERVES 9   **PREP TIME** 20 MINUTES   **SET TIME** 4 HOURS 10 MINUTES

Yoghurt bark is always trending online, so here is my favourite version of it. The apples add a juicy and crunchy tart flavour, whilst the cashew and coconut cream remain smooth and not icy, unlike frozen coconut yoghurt on its own.

APPLE CREAM
½ cup (75 g) raw cashews
1 cup (240 g) coconut yoghurt
½ cup vanilla protein powder
2 tablespoons rice malt syrup
1 teaspoon vanilla extract
dash of oat milk, if needed
2 pink lady apples, diced

CHOCOLATE TOPPING
80 g dark chocolate
1 tablespoon coconut oil
sea salt flakes, to sprinkle

1. For the apple cream, soak the cashews in boiling water for 10 minutes, then drain. Combine the coconut yoghurt, vanilla protein powder, rice malt syrup, vanilla extract and cashews in a food processor. Process until thick and smooth, adding a dash of oat milk if needed to process the cashews further. Pour into a bowl and mix in the diced apple.

2. Line a baking tray with baking paper and pour over the apple cream. Spread with the back of a spoon to create a rectangle of about 25 cm × 35 cm. Place in the freezer for 3–4 hours, to set.

3. To make the topping, place the chocolate and coconut oil into a small microwave-safe bowl. Microwave in 20-second increments, stirring between each, until fully melted. Alternatively, melt the chocolate and coconut oil on the stovetop in a double boiler.

4. Drizzle the melted chocolate over the apple cream and spread quickly with a spoon before it sets. Sprinkle with sea salt flakes and set in the freezer for a further 10 minutes. Cut into chards and serve.

TIP

Store in the freezer and remove 10 minutes before eating to soften slightly.

I am open to exploring new career paths and opportunities that excite and fulfil me.

mini banoffee pies.

MAKES 6 **PREP TIME** 30 MINUTES **SET TIME** 40 MINUTES

All the flavours of banana, coconut and caramel come together in these brilliant mini banoffee pies. They were one of the first no-bake recipes I experimented with when I went vegan, and they have come a long way since then to reach this drool-worthy result.

PIE SHELLS
2½ cups (300 g) almond meal
⅓ cup (40 g) vanilla protein powder
⅓ cup (80 g) coconut oil, melted
¼ cup (60 ml) rice malt syrup
1 teaspoon vanilla extract

ALMOND CARAMEL
¼ cup (65 g) almond butter
¼ cup (60 ml) rice malt syrup
2 tablespoons coconut oil, melted
1 teaspoon vanilla extract

GARNISH
½ cup (120 g) coconut yoghurt
1 banana, sliced
2 squares dark chocolate, shaved

1. To make the pie shells, combine the almond meal, vanilla protein powder and a pinch of salt in a large bowl and mix well. Add the melted coconut oil, rice malt syrup and vanilla extract. Mix with your hands until a dough forms. Divide into six equal balls.

2. Place one ball into each hole of a six-hole 7.5 × 4.5 cm capacity silicon muffin tray. Press down and shape into cups with your hands by creating a deep well in the centre. Set in the freezer for 20 minutes or until firm.

3. To make the almond caramel, place the almond butter, rice malt syrup, melted coconut oil, vanilla extract and a pinch of salt in a bowl. Mix until smooth.

4. Carefully pop the pie shells out of the muffin tray. Reserve about 1½ tablespoons of the almond caramel and spoon the rest into the shells, leaving about 1 cm of room at the top. Set in the freezer for a further 10 minutes.

5. Place 1 tablespoon coconut yoghurt and two banana slices on top of each. Add a teaspoon of reserved almond caramel, two more banana slices and some shaved dark chocolate. Set in the freezer for 10 minutes.

TIP

I recommend storing these pies in the fridge so that they are the perfect texture for eating straight away. However, they will last in the freezer for 2–3 weeks. Just remove 20–25 minutes before eating to thaw and soften.

With each new career endeavour, I am one step closer to living a life of purpose.

blueberry ice-cream bars.

SERVES 8 **PREP TIME** 20 MINUTES **SET TIME** 4 HOURS

These raw blueberry ice-cream bars make the perfect summer dessert. They are creamy, smooth and fruity. Keep them in the freezer but take them out about 20 minutes before eating to thaw slightly for the perfect texture.

BASE
4 Medjool dates, pitted
2 cups (240 g) almond meal
1 cup (100 g) walnuts
2 tablespoons almond butter
1 teaspoon ground cinnamon

FILLING
1½ cups (225 g) raw cashews
1 cup (240 g) coconut yoghurt
1 cup (140 g) frozen blueberries
⅓ cup (80 ml) rice malt syrup
juice of ½ lemon
1 teaspoon vanilla extract
dash of oat milk, if needed

TOPPING
2 cups (300 g) frozen blueberries
1½ tablespoons chia seeds
juice of ½ lemon
1 teaspoon vanilla extract

1. Line a freezer-safe container or loaf tin (about 24 cm × 14 cm × 7 cm) with baking paper, extending over the two long sides.

2. To make the base, soak the dates in boiling water for 5 minutes, then drain. Place into a food processor with the almond meal, walnuts, almond butter, cinnamon and a pinch of salt. Process until a fine and sticky dough forms. Transfer to the lined container and press with your hands to spread evenly over the base.

3. For the filling, soak the cashews in boiling water for 10 minutes, then drain. Place into a high-speed blender with the coconut yoghurt, frozen blueberries, rice malt syrup, lemon juice and vanilla extract. Blend until smooth and creamy. Add a touch of oat milk if needed to help your blender.

4. Pour the blueberry filling over the base and gently shake to even the top. Set in the freezer for 2 hours.

5. For the topping, combine the frozen blueberries, chia seeds, lemon juice and vanilla extract in a food processor and process until smooth. Dollop on top of the filling and smooth over with the back of a spoon. Set in the freezer for a further 2 hours.

6. Use the paper to lift out of the container. Cut into bars to serve.

TIP

When slicing, I recommend running your knife under hot water for a few minutes, drying it and then slicing to melt the ice-cream as you move the knife through.

I get to choose what career path I follow and don't live life purely to appease others.

mango matcha sorbet.

GF **OF** **RSF**

SERVES 3   **PREP TIME** 10 MINUTES   **FREEZE TIME** 3 HOURS

In my teenage years, I was obsessed with Boost Juice, a well-known smoothie chain in Australia. They had a flavour called Green Tea Mango Mantra that I just couldn't get enough of. Sadly, the flavour was discontinued. I never forgot just how good the flavours of green tea and mango were together, which is why I've brought both flavours back together in a sorbet version! It's the perfect light and refreshing dessert for hot summer days.

MANGO SORBET
3 cups (420 g) chopped frozen mango
2 tablespoons lemon juice

MATCHA SORBET
1 frozen banana
1 cup (140 g) chopped frozen mango
1½ teaspoon matcha powder

TO SERVE (OPTIONAL)
coconut yoghurt and fresh mango

1. To make the mango sorbet, place the frozen mango and lemon juice into a food processor or high-speed blender. Process until thick and smooth. Pour into a bowl and refrigerate until needed.

2. For the matcha sorbet, rinse out the food processor or high-speed blender and add the banana, frozen mango and matcha powder. Process until smooth.

3. Spoon dollops of the mango sorbet and matcha sorbet into an 2L capacity freezer-proof container. Smooth the top with the back of a spoon.

4. Place a lid on the container and freeze for 3 hours, or until firm.

5. To serve, use an ice-cream scoop to scoop the sorbet into bowls. If you like, top with coconut yoghurt and chunks of fresh mango.

TIP

Before scooping, I recommend running your ice-cream scoop under hot water for a few minutes to loosen up the sorbet as you scoop.

I release societal expectations or judgements about what a 'normal' career path should look like, and I follow my own path with confidence.

salted chocolate tahini fudge.

SERVES 12   **PREP TIME** 10 MINUTES   **SET TIME** 2 HOURS

This indulgent treat is a fusion of rich chocolate and creamy tahini. It has a gooey texture with a hint of salty and sesame undertones, adding depth to its sweetness. It's nut-free, refined sugar-free and incredibly easy to make.

FUDGE
¾ cup (180 ml) coconut milk
2 tablespoons tahini
2 tablespoons rice malt syrup
1 teaspoon vanilla extract
200 g dark chocolate, finely chopped

TOPPING
1 tablespoon tahini
1 teaspoon sesame seeds
¼ teaspoon sea salt flakes

1. To make the fudge, combine the coconut milk, tahini, rice malt syrup and vanilla extract in a saucepan. Heat over medium heat, stirring constantly, for 2 minutes or until hot. Add the chocolate and remove from the heat. Leave for 2 minutes to allow the chocolate to melt, then stir together until smooth.

2. Line a 20.5 cm square cake tin with baking paper, extending over two sides. Pour the chocolate mixture into the baking tray and gently shake to even out.

3. For the topping, scatter dollops of tahini over the fudge and swirl in with a skewer to create a marble pattern. Sprinkle over the sesame seeds and salt.

4. Place in the freezer for 1–2 hours, or until set.

5. Use the paper to lift out of the tray and cut into 12 pieces to serve.

TIP

Store in the fridge for the perfect gooey texture for eating, or store in the freezer and remove 20 minutes before eating.

I honour my inner calling to pursue a career that brings me joy and fulfilment.

baked desserts.

get baked, not serious.

Online dating. Boy, is that a tough nut to crack. One minute you think you're speaking to the dream dude and the next minute he has either fallen off the face of the Earth or bombarded you with a series of pictures you didn't expect and most definitely didn't want. Just when you think it couldn't get any worse, you check his profile only to find the clichéd phrase: 'I'm looking for someone who doesn't take themselves too seriously'. I kid you not when I say at least one-third of the guys on Hinge have it pinned to the top of their profile. Not only is the statement wishy-washy and hollow, but it always leaves me pondering: what exactly constitutes being 'too serious'? Is there some elusive 'too serious' rulebook I've missed? Do dudes have a checklist where they cross off boxes every time you present 'too serious' attributes? After going on a date with a 'too serious' box checker and asking him what he meant by it, I still didn't have a straight answer. I came to realise that most of these guys don't even know what the statement means themselves. So, as you do, I came up with my own definition. It's not about being reckless or selfish; rather, it's about embracing failure, finding humour in life's absurdities, extending forgiveness and nurturing love. It's about striving to be the happiest and most carefree versions of ourselves. With that in mind, for the final chapter of my book, I wanted to share some tips on how to adopt this 'not too serious' attitude.

1. **Fail more:** Ever tried wrapping your head around the size of the universe? According to Google, it spans a whopping 93 billion light-years in diameter. To put that into perspective, one light-year equals roughly 9.46 trillion kilometres. So, in the gentlest and most compassionate way possible, I can say that you don't even occupy the space in this universe that an ant does on Earth. In the grand scheme of things, all that we do doesn't really matter. Nothing really matters. I'm not saying this to encourage you to throw in the towel. You are still a living, breathing and powerful bundle of energetic mass. I'm saying this to let you know that it is okay to fail. In fact, it's not just ok, it's crucial for learning and growth. How else are we supposed to learn if something works or doesn't work if we don't at least try? Yes, failure can feel frustrating, embarrassing and upsetting in the moment. Know that those feelings are valid and normal. But as we move past our initial emotional reaction, we can observe where we went wrong and learn from it. Not taking life 'too seriously' is not caring about whether your next project, relationship, career, fill in the blank, will fail or succeed, but doing it anyway. Besides, consider this: failure and success don't exist. They are subjective constructs we choose to believe in. It's our perception of what constitutes either that shapes our interpretation of an outcome. So, why not just call everything a success? Burnt a loaf of banana bread? SUCCESS! Now you know to set the oven timer to 45 minutes instead of an hour next time.

2. **Laugh more:** When I first started posting online, I would cut every single mistake out of my cooking videos. Gosh, I couldn't be seen dropping food on the ground or splashing it all over my top. I'd look like a fraud! So, instead, I looked like a robot. Beep, boop, boooooooring. For my 22nd birthday, I wanted to post something special but had no content prepared. I did, however, have a full folder of blooper videos saved. So, giggling at myself all the way through making it, I cut and pasted all the bloopers together and posted it. That video received more comments than I had ever received on a video before. And at least 95% of them were positive

comments such as 'so relatable' or 'this makes me love you even more'. Birthday bloopers are now my trademark and I'll continue posting them every year as a reminder to laugh more. Laughing at our failures, or what we perceive to be failures, reminds us that nothing is that important. When we fail, the world keeps spinning, the sun keeps shining and you can choose to keep laughing. Plus, isn't it just so much easier to laugh at something than to worry about it? Laughing releases endorphins, relaxes us and puts us in a brighter headspace to think positive thoughts. Worrying makes us feel like crap. So, to live a life by the not 'too seriously' ethos, laugh as much as you possibly can.

3. **Forgive more:** We are all human. We have all had crappy things happen to us and have done crappy things to other people. I am not at all excusing how others have treated you in the past. But, allowing that to dictate your life is only going to affect you, not them. Let's say you were bullied in high school, and someone told you that you were ugly. Now every time you look in the mirror, get dressed up or take a photo, you think you look ugly. Do you think that person has even thought twice about that comment? They probably don't even remember saying it. So, who is actually doing the damage? You. You are the one giving life to that comment. You are the only person who can control your thoughts, feelings and beliefs. Thus, you are the only person that can think, feel and believe you are ugly. You cannot blame anyone else for this.

Forgiveness is taking responsibility for our lives and acknowledging that it is our own beliefs that have got us to where we are. If we want to move forward, we must stop giving power to the past and rewrite the narrative of who we are. We can choose to think exactly what we want to think. And as the saying goes, we become what we think. To forgive, you do not have to go up to a person who you feel has wronged you, give them a big hug and say 'I love and forgive you'. Unless, of course, that feels right for you. Simply writing a letter or a text message to express your forgiveness will do, even if you don't hit send. The very action of writing it to release it is cathartic enough. When we release a grudge, it can almost feel like a weight has been lifted off our shoulders.

For years I blamed my father, who wasn't in my life, for mum and I having little money. He didn't provide any financial support when I was growing up, so every time mum and I were struggling to afford this or that, I'd blame him. Not to his face, but in my head. Looking back, I can see how child, teenage and early adult Chloe used this as a coping mechanism. I am not at all going to excuse what he did. It was wrong and no father should abandon and treat their child like that. However, I was still blaming him even into my early adult years when I had financial independence. Still letting the narrative of an absent father halt my financial growth. Once I was able to forgive him for his lack of support through writing a letter to him, I was able to redirect my financial path. When I started working, I chose to believe I was rich and worthy of money and now that is my reality. Blaming is simply a way to make someone else responsible for issues that are of our own making.

When we acknowledge that we are all on our own path and doing the best we can with the knowledge and resources we have, this allows us to adopt a not 'too serious' attitude by releasing 'too serious' grudges. Forgiving doesn't mean allowing that person to re-enter your life with open arms. It just means accepting them for who they are, acknowledging their past actions and releasing the emotional strain those actions have on your life. And in case you were wondering, I did not send my father the letter. I am so content and grateful with my life that I don't feel the need to be in contact with him. However, I have forgiven him. I thank him for giving me the gift of life with the most loving and incredible mum to support me through it. If I can forgive, you can too.

4. **Love more:** I have the most beautiful, humorous and affectionate Chihuahua called Inka. She is tan in colour, weighs about 2 kg and somehow manages to run faster than I do with two coffees pumping through my veins. I often stare at Inka when she's asleep and all I can think about is how much I love her. I love her when she follows me around the house like a little shadow. I love her when she brings her favourite fluffy panda toy into bed every night. I even love her when she barks at the postie for dropping off a parcel at the doorstep which, when you're working in my industry, is almost every morning. I love her like a mother loves their child, unconditionally. I use the example of my dog because animals are just so easy to love. Many of us will have a pet or two or more of our own that bring us so much joy. What's amazing about love is that it makes us feel good. On a physical level, we release dopamine. This helps us to feel happier and adopt a more positive perspective on situations. Like loving your dog even when their barking is piercing your ear drums. But when we love, we also vibrate at a higher frequency. As like attracts like, we attract other people and situations also on the love frequency. These people and situations will give us more reason to love and so the cycle continues. Of course, we can't feel like a love machine every waking second. It's ok to feel flat when your pooch decides to have an accident on your bed. But the more love we can inject into our life, the better. When I was working with my life coach, I wrote a list of seven affirmations to repeat daily. Four of them, the majority, were focused on love: 'I experience love every day, love is all around me, I give and receive love equally and everything is love'. When we carry the belief that everything is love, we are in alignment with the not 'too serious' philosophy. We give love just as much as we receive it. We don't feel the need to fix, change or control everything as we can love it for what it already is.

When we fail, we learn. When we learn, we laugh. When we laugh, we feel high enough to forgive. And when we forgive, we can love. It's really that simple. Life is only as complicated as we make it. Having the ability to acknowledge that nothing is that important shifts us from a state of being careless to a state of being carefree. We can forgive and appreciate things as they are, without the need to change them. And, most importantly, we can think, move, speak and work using the energy of love and have that energy delivered straight back to us. Love is the definition of the not 'too serious' ethos.

This last chapter is the baking chapter. I'm not talking about baking in the smoking sense. This book teaches you how to cook with plants, just not those kinds of plants. However, I do believe that when we are in a love state, in a not 'too serious' state, we can feel high on life. Cooking for me is a love state, and baking even more so because the outcome is always sweet. So, line your baking trays, preheat that oven and get baked!

vanilla roasted plums with cinnamon cream.

SERVES 3   **PREP TIME** 10 MINUTES   **COOK TIME** 30 MINUTES

Mum and I used to have the cutest elderly neighbours who would very generously give us some of their juicy homegrown plums each week. I told them that one day I'd make a recipe with plums and dedicate it to them. So, here's a homage to juicy plums and, more importantly, kind neighbours.

ROASTED PLUMS
juice of ½ lemon
2 tablespoons rice malt syrup
1 teaspoon vanilla extract
½ teaspoon ground cinnamon
¼ teaspoon ground cardamom
6 black plums, halved and pitted
4 Medjool dates, pitted and chopped
1 tablespoon arrowroot flour

CINNAMON CREAM
1 cup (240 g) vanilla coconut yoghurt
2 tablespoons almond butter
1 tablespoon rice malt syrup
½ teaspoon vanilla extract
¼ teaspoon ground cinnamon

TO SERVE (OPTIONAL)
slivered almonds, toasted

1. Preheat the oven to 180°C.
2. For the roasted plums, place the lemon juice, rice malt syrup, vanilla extract, cinnamon, cardamom and a pinch of salt into a large bowl. Mix well, ensuring no clumps of cinnamon or cardamom remain. Add the plums, dates and arrowroot flour. Gently toss until evenly coated.
3. Transfer into a deep baking dish (about 24 cm square). Roast for 25–30 minutes, or until the plums are gel soft and any surrounding liquid has become jam-like.
4. Meanwhile, to make the cinnamon cream, combine the coconut yoghurt, almond butter, rice malt syrup, vanilla extract and cinnamon in a bowl. Whisk until smooth and well combined.
5. To serve, dollop the cinnamon cream onto plates and spread with the back of a spoon. Top with the roasted plums and spoon some of the jammy liquid on top. If you like, top with toasted slivered almonds.

TIP

You can substitute the plums with any small stone fruit of your choice. Some of my other favourites are peaches and apricots.

Forgiveness is a gift I give myself, allowing me to move forward with peace and compassion.

spiced sweet potato and olive oil cake.

SERVES 8   **PREP TIME** 25 MINUTES   **COOK TIME** 35 MINUTES + COOLING

Just because sweet potato, olive oil and tahini are typically savoury ingredients, does not mean they can't make for the most decadent dessert. This sweet potato cake is dense and fudgy like banana bread with the spiced flavour of a carrot cake. It's topped with a creamy cashew frosting and the most insane tahini caramel sauce.

CAKE
1 flax egg (1 tablespoon flaxseed meal and 2½ tablespoons water)
8 Medjool dates, pitted
2 cups (260 g) grated sweet potato
⅓ cup (80 ml) rice malt syrup
½ cup (125 ml) light olive oil
¾ cup (180 ml) soy milk
1 teaspoon vanilla extract
1¼ cups (170 g) gluten-free plain flour
1½ teaspoons ground cinnamon
½ teaspoon ground allspice
1 teaspoon baking powder

CASHEW FROSTING
1 cup (150 g) raw cashews
1 Medjool date, pitted
½ cup (125 ml) soy milk, plus more if needed
1 teaspoon vanilla extract
¼ teaspoon ground cinnamon

TAHINI CARAMEL
2 tablespoons tahini
2 tablespoons rice malt syrup
1–2 tablespoons soy milk, or as needed to thin
½ teaspoon vanilla extract

1. Preheat the oven to 180°C and line a 20 cm round cake tin.

2. To make the flax egg, place the flaxseed meal and water together in a small bowl and mix well. Allow to sit for 5 minutes.

3. For the cake, soak the dates in boiling water for 5 minutes, then drain and finely chop. Place the grated sweet potato, rice malt syrup, flax egg, olive oil, soy milk, vanilla extract and dates into a large bowl and mix well. Sift the flour, cinnamon, allspice, baking powder and a pinch of salt into the bowl and mix well. Pour into the greased cake tin and gently shake to even the top.

4. Bake for 30–35 minutes, or until the top is golden and a skewer comes out clean. Remove from the oven and allow to cool for 20 minutes. Remove from the cake tin and transfer to a wire rack to cool completely.

5. Meanwhile, for the cashew frosting, soak the cashews and the date in boiling water for 10 minutes. Place the cashews, date, soy milk, vanilla extract and cinnamon into a food processor. Process until smooth, stopping to scrape down the sides as needed. Add a dash more soy milk if needed to thin.

6. For the tahini caramel, mix the tahini, rice malt syrup, soy milk, vanilla extract and a pinch of salt in a small bowl until smooth.

7. To serve, spread the cashew frosting on top of the cake with the back of a spoon. Dollop over the tahini caramel and swirl through to create a marble pattern. Slice and serve.

With each failure, I become more resilient and determined to achieve my goals.

blueberry banana bread.

SERVES 8 **PREP TIME** 10 MINUTES **COOK TIME** 40 MINUTES

As a child, mum and I used to go to a local organic grocer every weekend and buy a fresh loaf of the fudgiest, sweetest and juiciest blueberry banana bread. Then one day that grocer stopped stocking the banana bread and my little 10-year-old heart broke into two pieces. Luckily, this banana bread tastes better than the original and glued those pieces straight back together.

1 cup (120 g) oat flour
1 cup (120 g) almond meal
1 teaspoon baking powder
1 teaspoon ground cinnamon
3 bananas, mashed
⅓ cup (95 g) peanut butter
⅓ cup (60 ml) rice malt syrup
1 teaspoon vanilla extract
⅓ cup (80 ml) oat milk
1 cup (140 g) frozen blueberries

1. Preheat the oven to 175°C and line the base of a 24 cm × 13 cm × 6.5 cm loaf tin with baking paper.
2. Place the oat flour, almond meal, baking powder, cinnamon and a pinch of salt into a large bowl and mix well.
3. Add the mashed banana, peanut butter, rice malt syrup, vanilla extract and oat milk. Mix until well combined. The mixture should be thick but pourable. Add a dash more oat milk if too thick.
4. Fold through the frozen blueberries and pour into the loaf tin. Bake for 35–40 minutes, or until the top is browned and a skewer comes out clean.
5. Remove from the oven and allow to cool for 20 minutes in the pan then turn out onto a wire rack to cool completely. Slice and serve.

TIP

Feel free to add different berries, nuts or seeds to this bread to mix up the flavours.

I celebrate my failures as valuable experiences that shape me into a stronger, wiser and more resilient individual.

roasted dates with pistachio butter.

SERVES 8   **PREP TIME** 20 MINUTES   **COOK TIME** 20 MINUTES

If you haven't tried roasted dates, then you are missing out! Roasting gives them a gooey burnt caramel flavour that pairs perfectly with the saltiness of pistachio butter and the creaminess of coconut yoghurt.

PISTACHIO BUTTER
2 cups (280 g) pistachio kernels

ROASTED DATES
16 Medjool dates, pitted
1 teaspoon ground cinnamon
1 teaspoon vanilla extract

TO SERVE
¼ cup (60 g) coconut yoghurt
2 tablespoons pistachio kernels, roughly chopped
2 tablespoons walnuts, roughly chopped
2 tablespoons rice malt syrup

1. Preheat the oven to 175°C. For the pistachio butter, spread pistachios onto a baking tray and roast for 8–10 minutes, mixing halfway through, or until golden. Remove from the oven and allow to cool.

2. Place the roasted pistachios into a food processor with a pinch of salt. Process on high for 10–12 minutes, stopping to scrape down the sides as needed, or until a smooth nut butter consistency forms.

3. Meanwhile, for the roasted dates, place the dates, cinnamon and vanilla extract into a large bowl and mix well.

4. Line a baking tray with baking paper. Arrange the dates onto the tray and roast for 10 minutes, or until they are gooey and hot. Remove from the oven.

5. To serve, dollop the coconut yoghurt onto plates and spread with the back of a spoon. Add a few teaspoons of the pistachio butter and spread with a spoon to create a marbled pattern. Top with the dates and add a few more teaspoons of pistachio butter on top. Sprinkle with chopped pistachios and walnuts and drizzle over the rice malt syrup.

TIPS

The dates are best eaten warm out of the oven. If storing leftover dates in the fridge, I recommend heating them in the oven at 175°C for 3–5 minutes, or in the microwave for 20–30 seconds to soften them.

I find balance by not allowing seriousness to overshadow the joy of the present moment.

chunky chickpea cookies.

MAKES 10   **PREP TIME** 20 MINUTES   **COOK TIME** 30 MINUTES + COOLING

Chickpea flour is super underrated. Not only does it have a subtle taste that is easily covered in sweet recipes, but it packs a mean amount of protein in comparison to regular flour. These cookies have an irresistible cake-like consistency with a golden crunch on the outside.

1½ cups (180 g) almond meal
1¼ cups (185 g) chickpea flour
⅓ cup (40 g) vanilla protein powder
1 teaspoon baking powder
1 cup (250 ml) oat milk
½ cup (130 g) almond butter
⅓ cup (80 ml) rice malt syrup
1 teaspoon vanilla extract
1 cup (120 g) frozen raspberries
⅓ cup (65 g) dark chocolate chips
3 Medjool dates, pitted and chopped

1. Preheat oven to 175°C and line a large baking tray with baking paper.
2. Place the almond meal, chickpea flour, vanilla protein powder, baking powder and a pinch of salt into a large bowl and mix well.
3. Add the oat milk, almond butter, rice malt syrup and vanilla extract and mix until well combined. The mixture should be on the thick and stickier side. Fold through the raspberries, chocolate chips and chopped dates.
4. Dollop the mixture onto the baking tray to create 10 cookies. Use damp hands to flatten and shape the cookies and bake for 30 minutes, or until the tops and edges are golden.
5. Remove from the oven and allow to cool on the tray for 10 minutes to firm up.

TIP

You can use this cookie base for any cookie flavour! For example, if you fancy a chocolate and blueberry cookie, substitute the vanilla protein powder for chocolate protein powder or cocoa powder and swap the raspberries for blueberries.

*I am worthy of love in all its forms and frequently express it to others.
I attract loving relationships into my life effortlessly.*

cheat's tiramisu.

SERVES 8   **PREP TIME** 20 MINUTES   **COOK TIME** 30 MINUTES + COOLING   **SET TIME** 3 HOURS

This cheat's tiramisu is healthier, higher in protein and, of course, plant-based. It is by no means traditional, but it requires less time and effort and still tastes incredible.

CAKE
4 Medjool dates, pitted
2 cups (240 g) oat flour
1 cup (120 g) almond meal
1 teaspoon baking powder
1¼ cup (310 ml) soy milk
¼ cup (60 ml) rice malt syrup
1 teaspoon vanilla extract

CREAM
½ cup (75 g) raw cashews
1 cup (240 g) coconut yoghurt
⅓ cup (40 g) vanilla protein powder
2 tablespoons rice malt syrup
1 teaspoon vanilla extract

TO ASSEMBLE
1 cup (250 ml) strong black coffee
2 teaspoons cacao powder, for dusting

1. Preheat oven to 175°C and line a 20.5 cm square cake tin with baking paper.

2. To make the cake, soak the dates in boiling water for 5 minutes, then drain and mash. Place the oat flour, almond meal, baking powder and a pinch of salt into a large bowl and mix well.

3. Add the dates, soy milk, rice malt syrup and vanilla extract. Mix until thick and well combined. The mixture should be scoopable but not runny. Add a dash more oat milk if too thick and a touch more oats if too runny. Pour into the baking tray and smooth the surface with the back of a spoon.

4. Bake for 25–30 minutes, or until a skewer comes out clean. Allow to cool then slice into 12 rectangles.

5. Meanwhile, for the cream, soak the cashews in boiling water for 10 minutes, then drain. Place the coconut yoghurt, vanilla protein powder, rice malt syrup, vanilla extract and the cashews into a food processor. Process until smooth, stopping to scrape down the sides as needed.

6. To assemble the tiramisu, dip half of the cake rectangles into the coffee and gently turn a few times to soak. Lay over the base of a rectangular dish (see tip) and press down softly to push to the edges. Spread half the cream over. Repeat with the remaining cake and cream. Set in the fridge for 3 hours.

7. Remove from the fridge, dust with cacao powder, slice and serve.

TIP

I used a 2L, 24 cm × 12 cm dish to layer the tiramisu. For best results, I recommend using a similar sized container.

Love is my natural state of being and I express it freely to myself and others.

strawberry shortcake trifles.

SERVES 6　**PREP TIME** 15 MINUTES　**COOK TIME** 30 MINUTES + COOLING　**SET TIME** 3 HOURS

This is one of those desserts that you could eat every single night and never get tired of. It's layered with a sweet and fudgy vanilla cake, decadent cashew cream and sliced strawberries. The best part of all, it contains zero added sweeteners or oils!

CAKE
2 Medjool dates, pitted,
2¼ cups (200 g) rolled oats
1 cup (120 g) almond meal
1 teaspoon baking powder
1 small banana, mashed
6 large strawberries, mashed
1 teaspoon vanilla extract
1¼ cup (310 ml) oat milk

CREAM
½ cup (75 g) raw cashews
5 Medjool dates, pitted
1 cup (240 g) coconut yoghurt
⅓ cup (40 g) vanilla protein powder
1 teaspoon vanilla extract
½ cup (125 ml) oat milk

TO SERVE
18 strawberries, halved
2 teaspoons ground cinnamon, for dusting

1. Preheat the oven to 175°C and line a 24 cm square cake tin with baking paper.

2. To make the cake, soak the dates in boiling water for 5 minutes, then drain and mash. Place the oats, almond meal, baking powder and a pinch of salt into a large bowl and mix well.

3. Add the dates, banana, strawberries, vanilla extract and oat milk. Mix until thick and well combined. The mixture should be scoopable but not runny. Add a dash more oat milk if too thick and a touch more oats if too runny. Pour the mixture into the baking tray and smooth the top with the back of a spoon.

4. Bake for 25–30 minutes, or until a skewer comes out clean. Allow to cool for 15 minutes. Remove from the tray and allow to cool completely. Slice into 2 cm cubes.

5. For the cream, soak the cashews and dates in boiling water. Take out the dates after 5 minutes, then soak the cashews for 5 more minutes. Drain. Place the coconut yoghurt, vanilla protein powder, vanilla extract, oat milk, dates and cashews into a food processor. Process until smooth.

6. Divide ½ the cake cubes among 6 glasses or jars. Spoon over ½ the cream and top each with three strawberry halves. Repeat, layering the remaining cake, cream and strawberries. Set in the fridge for 3 hours.

7. Dust with cinnamon to serve.

TIP

If you prefer things a little sweeter, feel free to add 1–2 tablespoons of your choice of liquid sweetener to the cake and cream.

I embrace laughter as a powerful force for joy and healing in my life.

choc brownies with avocado frosting.

SERVES 9   **PREP TIME** 10 MINUTES   **COOK TIME** 30 MINUTES + COOLING

This is my healthy alternative to a traditional brownie. It's fudgy, easy to make and topped with the smoothest and most decadent avocado frosting. I love serving it with fresh berries for an extra burst of sweetness.

BROWNIE
1 chia egg (1 tablespoon chia seeds and 2 ½ tablespoons water)
4 Medjool dates, pitted
2 cups (240 g) oat flour
1 cup (120 g) almond meal
¼ cup (25 g) cacao powder
1 teaspoon baking powder
¼ cup (70 g) peanut butter
¼ cup (60 ml) rice malt syrup
1 teaspoon vanilla extract
1 ¼ cup (310 ml) oat milk
¼ cup (45 g) dark chocolate chips

FROSTING
1 ripe avocado
¼ cup (25 g) cacao powder
¼ cup (60 ml) rice malt syrup
¼ cup (60 g) coconut yoghurt
½ teaspoon vanilla extract

TO SERVE (OPTIONAL)
fresh berries

1. Preheat the oven to 175°C and line a 24 cm square cake tin with baking paper.

2. To make the chia egg, place the chia seeds and water in a small bowl and mix well. Allow to sit for 5 minutes.

3. To make the brownie, soak the dates in boiling water for 5 minutes, then drain and mash. Place the oat flour, almond meal, cacao powder, baking powder and a pinch of salt into a large bowl and mix well.

4. Add the dates, peanut butter, rice malt syrup, chia egg, vanilla extract and oat milk. Mix until well combined. The mixture should be thick but scoopable. Add a dash more oat milk if needed. Add the chocolate chips and mix through. Pour the batter into the baking tray and smooth the surface with the back of a spoon.

5. Bake for 25–30 minutes, or until the top has browned and a skewer comes out clean. Set aside to cool for 15 minutes. Remove from the tray and allow to cool completely.

6. Meanwhile, to make the frosting, place the avocado, cacao powder, rice malt syrup, coconut yoghurt, vanilla extract and a pinch of salt into a food processor. Process until thick and smooth. Add an extra dash of oat milk if you think it is too thick.

7. Dollop the frosting over the brownies and spread with a spoon. Slice and, if you like, serve topped with fresh berries.

TIP

The frosting is also delicious on its own as a chocolate mousse alternative.

I recognise that holding onto a grudge only poisons my own life, so I choose to forgive for my own wellbeing.

raspberry crumble.

SERVES 8 **PREP TIME** 10 MINUTES **COOK TIME** 35 MINUTES

Peanut butter and jam together are like a match made in foodie heaven, and when you pop them into a crumble, it's pure magic. With peanut butter already packing its own natural oils, the crumble gets beautifully golden and crunchy without needing to add any extra oil.

BASE
5 cups (600 g) frozen raspberries
5 Medjool dates, pitted and chopped
juice of ½ lemon
1 teaspoon vanilla extract

CRUMBLE
2 cups (180 g) rolled oats
¼ cup (30 g) vanilla protein powder
1 teaspoon ground cinnamon
½ cup (140 g) peanut butter
¼ cup (60 ml) rice malt syrup
1½ tablespoons oat milk, plus more if needed
1 teaspoon vanilla extract

TO SERVE (OPTIONAL)
vanilla coconut yoghurt and fresh raspberries

1. Preheat the oven to 175°C and lightly grease a 2L glass baking dish.
2. For the base, place the frozen raspberries, dates, lemon juice and vanilla extract into the baking dish. Mix well.
3. For the crumble, place the rolled oats, vanilla protein powder and cinnamon into a bowl and mix well. Add the peanut butter, rice malt syrup, oat milk and vanilla extract. Mix with your hands until thick and clumpy. Add a dash more oat milk if it seems too dry.
4. Sprinkle the crumble over the berry base. Bake for 30–35 minutes, or until the raspberries are gooey and the crumble is golden and crisp.
5. Spoon into serving bowls. If you like, serve with coconut yoghurt and fresh raspberries.

TIP

Feel free to substitute the frozen raspberries and peanut butter for any other berry or nut butter. For example, another favourite of mine is frozen blueberries and almond butter.

I release resentment and choose to forgive, freeing myself from the burden of the past.

easy cinnamon scrolls.

SERVES 12   **PREP TIME** 20 MINUTES   **COOK TIME** 30 MINUTES

These no-rise, oil-free and sweetener-free cinnamon scrolls are incredible! The dough contains only three ingredients, banana, coconut yoghurt and self-raising flour. Making them simple to create and budget-friendly.

DOUGH
1 banana, mashed
¾ cup (180 g) vanilla coconut yoghurt
2⅓ cups (350 g) self-raising flour, plus more for rolling

FILLING
5 Medjool dates, pitted
¼ cup (65 g) almond butter
¼ cup (60 ml) oat milk
2 teaspoons ground cinnamon, plus more for dusting

ICING
¼ cup (60 g) vanilla coconut yoghurt
1 tablespoon oat milk
1 teaspoon vanilla extract

1. Preheat oven to 180°C and line a 20.5 cm square cake tin with baking paper.

2. For the dough, place the mashed banana and coconut yoghurt into a large bowl and mix well. Add the flour, ½ cup (75 g) at a time, and mix with your hands until a dough forms. If the dough is too wet, add more flour and if the dough is too dry, add more yoghurt.

3. Lightly flour a work surface and place the dough on top. Knead until smooth and roll into a rectangle shape (roughly 40 cm × 25 cm) with a rolling pin. The thickness should be roughly 1–1.5 cm.

4. To make the filling, soak the dates in boiling water for 5 minutes, then drain and mash. Combine in a small bowl with the almond butter, oat milk, cinnamon and a pinch of salt. Mix well. Dollop on top of the dough and spread evenly with the back of a spoon. Dust a light layer of extra cinnamon on top.

5. Starting on a long side, roll the dough tightly into a log shape. Cut into 12 equal slices. Place the rolls into the baking dish cut side down and press each down with your hands to squish slightly.

6. Bake for 25–30 minutes or until golden on top and a skewer comes out clean. Remove from the oven and allow to cool for 5 minutes.

7. Meanwhile, for the icing, place the coconut yoghurt, oat milk and vanilla extract into a small bowl. Mix well and drizzle over the rolls.

TIP

Store any leftovers in the fridge for 4–5 days. Reheat in a 180°C oven for 5 minutes before eating.

I embrace the joy of living by not taking life too seriously.

reference.

sample meal & mind plan.

Having recipes and self-development tools is one thing but incorporating them into your life is another. We are creatures of habit and will continue living the same life day in and day out unless we make a conscious effort to change it. That's why I wanted to give you this sample two-week meal and mind plan. For the next 14 days, your goal is to focus on eating healthy, plant-based meals and incorporating at least two mindfulness activities into each day. I have created a plan that lays everything out for you in the most straightforward way possible and even has a box for you to check at the end of the day. Because there is nothing more satisfying than checking a circle when a task is completed. I have included some of my favourite recipes from the book in this plan, but feel free to substitute any of the other recipes from that category. For example, you could swap out the peanut soba noodle stir fry for the creamy green pasta.

As most of my recipes serve between two and five people, you are more than welcome to share the meals with others. In fact, I encourage doing the whole plan with other people. You can motivate one another and hold each other accountable for each task and recipe. However, if you live by yourself and choose to do it on your own, that's ok too! You will have lots of leftovers, so I recommend finishing those off before moving on to the next meal. You can even freeze some dishes for meal prep to enjoy later. I have repeated some of the breakfast, lunch and snack options throughout both weeks as these are the recipes I recommend meal prepping at the start of the week.

The goal here is to show that cooking healthy plant-based recipes does not have to be hard or time-consuming. Neither do mindfulness activities. It will, however, make you feel clearer, fresher, more positive and focused. Whilst this challenge is only 14 days, it is my hope that afterwards, you continue to introduce some of these plant-based recipes or mindfulness activities into your life as you see fit. Listen to your body, see what works and have fun with it.

Let's gooooooooo.

week 1.

	MONDAY	TUESDAY	WEDNESDAY
BREAKFAST	Peanut butter & jam overnight oats	Peanut butter & jam overnight oats	Smoky baked beans
Mindfulness activity one	Write a mind map outlining all you want to manifest in your life. Be as specific and detailed as you can, including timelines or quantifiable targets for each aspiration. Pin that mind map to your bathroom mirror, wardrobe or somewhere where you'll see it often. The more you see it, the more reinforcement and motivation it will provide.	As soon as you wake up, go outside and stand on the ground. Preferably stand on a grass surface with no shoes on. This practice, known as grounding, establishes an electrical connection between you and the Earth. It is believed to foster relaxation and alleviate various physical and mental ailments.	Google search a personal values test on your phone. Complete the test and write down your top five values. Next to each brainstorm ideas to further integrate that value into your daily life. For example, if you value family, an idea could be scheduling a family dinner with your mum every Wednesday. This exercise fosters self-awareness as it allows you to visually understand how you can begin to live more in alignment with your values.
LUNCH	Tex Mex salad	Tex Mex salad	Broccolini and crispy tempeh salad
DINNER	Simple tofu curry	Nut-free mac and cheese	Eggy nasi goreng
SNACKS/ SWEETS	Chickpea tuna mousse crostini	Apple cream bark	Chickpea tuna mousse crostini
Mindfulness activity two	Engage in a body scan. Lie on your back with your legs extended and arms at your side. Mindfully focus your attention on each part of your body, working from the crown of your head all the way to the tip of your toes. Throughout the practice, maintain awareness of your breath and bodily sensations, no matter how big or small.	Find a quiet space, set an alarm for 10 to 30 minutes and choose your favourite book. Read, read and read some more. Immerse yourself in the pages and allow the words to transport you to a new realm of imagination. This will help to spark your creativity and allow you to learn something new to take into the week.	Go for a 30-minute evening sunset walk. Pay attention to each step. Feel the ground beneath you. Notice the movement of your body. Listen to the sounds and observe your surroundings without any judgement.
	Completed ○	Completed ○	Completed ○

week 1.

THURSDAY	FRIDAY	SATURDAY	SUNDAY
Smoky baked beans	Mocha hazelnut smoothie	Spicy tofu scramble breakfast tacos	Baked bananas with blueberry sauce
Set an alarm for 10 minutes and position yourself in front of a mirror. Stare at your reflection, maintaining full eye contact. Investigate all your features, your eyes, mouth, nose, skin and beyond. Allow any thoughts or emotions to flow naturally, refraining from any judgement of those thoughts. Once the 10 minutes is over, record everything you experienced. Delve into the origins of those thoughts and emotions. Why did they surface? What do they reveal about your self-perception?	Craft an 'I can' list. This involves identifying all the areas in which you are currently harbouring self-doubt and transforming each 'can't' into an empowering affirmation of capability. For example: Can't: I can't pursue my passion and turn it into a successful career. Can: I can pursue my passion and turn it into a successful career by setting goals, prioritising my time and staying committed to my vision.	Search for a 30-minute yoga or Pilates flow on YouTube. If you are a beginner, perhaps adding beginner to your search is a good place to start. Once you've selected a video that stands out for you, begin the practice. Focus your attention on your breath and how your body feels as you work through each movement.	Take yourself on a coffee date to your favourite local café and leave your phone at home. It might feel scary or odd going alone. However, it is a great way to build confidence, strength and appreciation for yourself as you grow comfortable being in your own company.
Broccolini and crispy tempeh salad	Beetroot and cucumber bowl	Roasted eggplant with creamy slaw bowl	Roasted eggplant with creamy slaw bowl
Miso carrot pasta	Gochujang tofu burger	Thai green curry	Traybake tacos
Apple cream bark	Easy cinnamon scrolls	Spicy capsicum and walnut dip and veggie sticks	Easy cinnamon scrolls
Think of one person in your life who you feel has wronged you. Open your journal and write them a letter of forgiveness. You never have to send it to them, the very act of writing it can be cathartic and healing enough. End the letter with 'I love and forgive you'.	Invite a few friends over to enjoy dinner with. Focus on listening to your friends and living in the present, avoiding checking your phone. Be open to different ideas and opinions. Laugh at every possible opportunity.	If you were given a large sum of money, what would you do with it? For this activity, I want you to write down all the things you would do in life if financial constraints didn't exist. When we eliminate barriers we perceive to be limiting us, we unlock the freedom to explore our deepest desires and clarify our priorities. For instance, if you write down 'leave my current job and start my own business', consider it a sign to take action. Every step, no matter how incremental, brings you closer to realising your dreams.	Open your journal and take a few moments to reflect on the past week. Capture the highlights, recounting the moments that brought you joy and gratitude. Take note of the challenges you faced, acknowledging the lessons they imparted and the growth they facilitated. By embracing both the triumphs and trials, you pave the way for personal development and resilience.
Completed ○	Completed ○	Completed ○	Completed ○

week 2.

	MONDAY	TUESDAY	WEDNESDAY
BREAKFAST	Mini pesto eggless frittata	Mini pesto eggless frittata	Miso date caramel smoothie
Mindfulness activity one	Write a list of 20 things that you are grateful for. Start each sentence with 'I am grateful for...' and go into detail with each point. For example, instead of 'I am grateful for healthy food.' It could be 'I am grateful for the ability to stock my fridge with fresh fruit and vegetables because they energise and nourish my body.'	Count 10 breaths. Begin by finding a space to sit quietly. Focus your attention on your breath. Beginning at one, inhale, hold your breath for three seconds and exhale. Notice your stomach filling up with each inhale and releasing with each exhale. If your mind wanders and you lose count, gently bring your focus back to your breath and begin again. This small but powerful practice will calm your nervous system and enhance concentration.	Find a space where you are alone and won't be seen or disturbed. Pick your favourite upbeat song and for the entire length of the song, dance. Make your moves as big, wild and free as you can. This activity will evoke laughter, release tension and flood your system with endorphins to leave you feeling invigorated.
LUNCH	Orange and sesame noodle salad	Orange and sesame noodle salad	Black rice and rocket salad
DINNER	Sweet potato and rice traybake	Marry me gnocchi	Rainbow peanut noodles
SNACKS/ SWEETS	Banana blueberry bread	Roast garlic hummus and veggie sticks	Banana blueberry bread
Mindfulness activity two	Before falling asleep, close your eyes in bed. Envision exactly how you want tomorrow to go from start to finish. What will you do in the morning? What conversations will you have? How will you move your body? And, most importantly, what will you eat (hint, it's listed in the next column)?	Grab a blank piece of paper and a pen. Set an alarm for 1 minute, close your eyes and free draw. Allow your intuition to guide the pen. Once the minute is over, open your eyes and see if there are any shapes or patterns that hold meaning for you. You might like to continue drawing to add detail to those shapes or patterns or simply appreciate them as they are.	Think of one person in your life who you are grateful for. Open your journal and write them a letter expressing your love, appreciation and gratitude for them in detail. Focus on the act of writing and the emotions it evokes, allowing yourself to fully connect with the sentiment behind each word. End the letter with 'I love you'.
	Completed ○	Completed ○	Completed ○

week 2.

THURSDAY	FRIDAY	SATURDAY	SUNDAY
Snickez oatmeal	Strawberries and cream smoothie	Smashed avocado and garlic mushrooms on toast	The best acai bowl
Google search for a random word generator online. Generate a word and then challenge yourself to create an affirmation using it. This activity encourages you to shift your perspective and find empowerment in unexpected places. For example, if the generated word is 'challenge', you could create the 'I embrace challenges as opportunities for growth and transformation'. Write this affirmation down on a sticky note and stick it to your computer screen, in your wallet or somewhere where you'll see it multiple times in the day.	Look through old childhood photos and select one that speaks to you. Perhaps it evokes a thought, memory or emotion. Whilst looking at that image, engage in a conversation with your inner child, whether in your head or out loud. Ask them what they need and offer them comfort and support. Remind them of their inherent worth and how much they are loved.	Make lunch for a family member or close friend. Turn off your phone so you can be attentive and fully present with them. Let your family member or friend know how much you love and appreciate them.	Write a letter to your future self in a year's time. Mention how proud you are of achieving the goals you are currently working towards. Express gratitude for your creativity, intelligence, beauty, intuition and growth. Hide the letter somewhere safe where only you know its location. Set a reminder on your phone for a year's time to open it.
Black rice and rocket salad	Mustardy potato salad	Mustardy potato salad	Half roasted cauliflower bowl
Traybake tacos	BBQ mushroom flatbreads	Carrot noodle soup	The best (ever) vegan nachos
Roast garlic hummus and veggie sticks	Peanut butter cookie protein balls	Roasted dates with pistachio butter.	Peanut butter cookie protein balls
Search for bedtime yoga on YouTube and pick a video to follow just before you hop into bed. Remember to breathe, focus on the movement and observe the way your body feels.	Create a vision board for the next three months. I recommend making a tangible one by printing off images and words and pinning them to a canvas board. Alternatively, you can utilise apps or websites such as Canva to create a virtual version to save as your iPhone or laptop screen. However, I highly encourage printing off a physical copy as well to hang in a location where you'll see it regularly.	Take yourself on an early evening drive and leave your phone at home. Pull over and park the car when your intuition tells you to. Watch and observe everything around you. Sit in silence and appreciate living in the present.	Book something spontaneous to do within the next month. Step outside of your comfort zone and choose an activity that you wouldn't typically involve yourself in. This could be booking an art class, a motivational speaker's workshop or joining a run club. Embrace the opportunity to explore different experiences, meet people and learn something new.

Completed ○   Completed ○   Completed ○   Completed ○

conversion chart.

The difference between measuring cups and spoons varies slightly from country to country. However, the difference is generally not enough to affect the cooking result. All cup and spoon measurements are level. One Australian metric measuring cup holds 250 ml, one Australian metric tablespoon holds 20 ml and one Australian teaspoon holds 5 ml. North America, New Zealand and the United Kingdom use a 15 ml tablespoon. Oven temperatures in this book are also for conventional ovens. If you use a fan-forced oven, reduce the temperature by 10 to 20 degrees Celsius.

DRY MEASUREMENTS

metric (g)	imperial (oz)
15	½
30	1
60	2
125	4
185	6
250	8
375	12
500	16
1000	32

LIQUID MEASUREMENTS

cup	metric (ml)	imperial (fl oz)
⅛	30	1
¼	60	2
⅓	80	2 and ½
½	125	4
⅔	160	5
¾	180	6
1	250	8
2	500	16
2 and ¼	560	20
4	1000	32

LENGTH MEASURES

Metric (cm)	Imperial (inches)
0.3	⅛
0.6	¼
1	½
2.5	1
5	2
18	7
20	8
23	9
25	10
30	12

OVEN TEMPERATURES

°c	°f	gas mark
120	250	½
150	300	2
170	325	3
180	350	4
190	375	5
200	400	6
220	425	7
230	450	8

conclusion.

By the time this book is released, I will be almost 24 years old. Meaning, quite obviously, I have a lot of life left to live. I have so much more to learn, grow and give back to this world. But I hope that from my 24 years of learning, I have been able to give you something in this book to take away, whether it be a delicious recipe or a self-development tool. I can't wait to share with you all my new recipes and insights when I'm 30 years old, 50 years old, or better yet, 100 years old. Yep, I said it. I will be a centenarian. Now that it's out in the open and published in writing, you can hold me accountable. There is one final story I want to leave you with before I conclude this book. Something so special that I have saved it for last.

When I went full-time into content creation and recipe development in 2021, I wrote a big manifestation mind map of all the things I wanted to achieve. I wanted to reach, inspire and help as many people as possible. I wanted to see people sharing and recreating my recipes every day. And, my biggest goal, I wanted to write a cookbook. But not just any cookbook. I wanted to write one that had just as much of a focus on mindset as it did on food. Health is multifaceted and I wanted a book that held mental and emotional health to the same value as physical health. The most shocking part of all, within that manifestation mind map and other manifestation mind maps I had written years prior (including when I was in primary school), I always wrote the name of one publisher: Penguin Random House. As a child, I was obsessed with the little white and black penguin on the vibrant orange books. And as a teenager, I went through a phase where they were the only books I'd buy just for the aesthetic. So, in a sense, Penguin books have been with me through all the stages of my life, and I couldn't think of anyone I wanted to publish my first book with more.

A mere three years later, on a sunny Spring afternoon when I was least expecting it, I received a small but life-changing message in my Instagram DMs. It was from a Penguin Random House Australia editor. To make it even more crazy, the first time I jumped on a Zoom call with the Penguin team, I discovered that Ashwin, the editor of this very book, not only used to live a few streets down from me but was once a teacher at my high school before I attended. My mind was officially blown.

I wanted to conclude the book with this story to show that anything is possible. I know how cliché that sounds, so feel free to roll your eyes. But it doesn't take away from the fact that it is true. Ten-year-old Chloe reading from her little orange Penguin books dreamed of writing her own book with that same publisher. Thirteen years later and she has done it. Don't know why I decided to speak in the third person for the last sentence. Perhaps it gives a more dramatic effect. But, back to my point. If you want something badly enough, that something will happen when the time is right. The universe is always working for your higher good. It loves you. And I love you too.

acknowledgements.

Firstly, I want to say thank you to my best friend and biggest supporter, mum. This book is just as much mine as it is yours. You have gone above and beyond as a mother, always putting me first, supporting my dreams and encouraging me to take every opportunity. I cannot thank you enough for your help during the whole process of this book. In particular, the photoshoot, where you worked tirelessly to conquer the mountain of dishes, take hundreds of behind-the-scenes snaps and taste the food (of course). You are the strongest, wisest and most giving woman I have ever met, and you inspire me every day. I told my teacher in prep that I wanted to be just like you when I grew up, and I can say with my whole heart that I still do. I love you!

A heartfelt thank you to all the team at Penguin Random House Australia. You don't understand how excited child Chloe would be knowing that she did write a book with her dream publisher:

- To Ashwin Khurana, the commissioning editor, thank you for believing in me! I am so grateful for your support and guidance throughout the entire process of this book. It was lovely to meet you during the photoshoot and again on a visit to Sydney at the Penguin Random House Australia HQ. A further thank you to Tracy Rutherford for editorial support.
- A big thank you to Kirby Armstrong for the stunning design of this book. It is even more beautiful than I had imagined!
- Thank you to my publicist Lily Crozier and marketer Madison Du for being so fun to work with, championing this book and pushing it out in the world in every which way possible.

Next up, a big and squishy hug to all involved in the photoshoot. It was a massive 10 days, and I wouldn't have gotten through it without such a supportive, creative and proactive team:

- Firstly, to Sammy Green and Meryl Batlle, my photographer and food stylist, you were the dream team. It was such a pleasure working with two kind and professional people. You are both so talented at your crafts and have a solution for everything. Each shot in this book is so effortlessly beautiful, clean and vivid, just as I'd hoped it would look. Thank you for bringing my recipes to life.
- To Paul, Carrie, Stella and Ruby Spano who let me use their stunning kitchen, thank you. There are not many friends who would be generous enough to let me cause chaos in their kitchen for 10 days without a single complaint. You were all so supportive and interested in the whole process even when your kitchen looked like a tornado had passed through it. Thank you for being a big part of my first-ever cookbook. I am so grateful.

Lastly, I wanted to say a massive thank you to YOU. If you purchased this book, thank you. If you were gifted this book, thank you. If you found this book on the side of the damn road, thank you. The very fact that you are currently holding this book is enough to fill my heart. I feel so grateful each and every day to be able to connect, help and inspire so many beautiful people with my recipes. The constant love and support I receive across all my social media accounts is so touching and I honestly would not be where I am today, writing a cookbook, without you. So, again, thank you.

index.

a
acai
    the best acai bowl 29
almond caramel 186
apple cream 185
    apple cream bark 185
artichoke
    butter bean and artichoke dip 55
avocado
    avocado and garlic mushrooms on toast 22
    avocado crema 94
    choc brownies with avocado frosting 214
    guacamole 140

b
baked bananas with blueberry sauce 25
baked potato wedges with BBQ sauce 60
balsamic dressing 93
bananas
    baked bananas with blueberry sauce 25
    blueberry banana bread 205
    mini banoffee pies 186
basil
    chunky pesto 55
    polenta caprese salad 89
BBQ mushroom flatbreads 156
BBQ sauce 60
beans, black
    chilli beans 140
    spiced corn and beans 94
    tray bake tacos 123
beans, white
    beetroot whip 78
    butter bean and artichoke dip 55
    butter bean Caesar 90
    golden butter bean stew 139
    miso bean mash 156
    smoky baked beans 33
    smoky butter beans 90
beetroot
    beetroot and cucumber bowl 78
    beetroot whip 78
    pink beetroot hummus 52

best acai bowl 29
best (ever) vegan nachos 140
black rice and rocket salad 93
blueberries
    blueberry banana bread 205
    blueberry ice-cream bars 189
    blueberry sauce 25
bounty baked oats 30
bowls
    beetroot and cucumber bowl 78
    falafel mezze bowl 82
    roasted cauliflower bowl 85
    roasted eggplant with creamy slaw bowl 77
    the best acai bowl 29
bread, blueberry banana 205
broccolini
    broccolini and crispy tempeh salad 97
    pan-fried broccolini and peas 97
brothy coconut noodles 163
brownies
    choc brownies with avocado frosting 214
burger
    gochujang tofu burger 147
butter beans
    butter bean and artichoke dip 55
    butter bean Caesar 90
    golden butter bean stew 139
    miso bean mash 156
    smoky butter beans 90
butternut pumpkin risoni 107

c
cabbage slaw 77
cacao nibs
    mint choc chip smoothie 45
Caesar dressing 90
cake
    cake (cheat's tiramisu) 210
    cake (strawberry shortcake trifles) 213
    no-bake carrot cake 173
    spiced sweet potato and olive oil cake 202

capsicum
    capsicum sauce 85
    romanesco sauce 164
    spicy capsicum and walnut dip 54
    sweet potato and capsicum soup 127
caramel
    almond caramel 186
    nutty caramel slice 182
    salted caramel and coconut protein balls 177
    tahini caramel 202
carrots
    carrot noodle soup 144
    miso carrot pasta 120
    no-bake carrot cake 173
    roasted carrots on whipped tofu 67
cashews
    cashew frosting 202
    cashew queso 56
    cheese 59
    simple cashew cream 57
    spicy cashew cream 26
cauliflower
    cauliflower floret focaccia sandwich 164
    roasted cauliflower bowls 85
cheat's dhal 159
cheat's tiramisu 210
cheese 59
cheesy breakfast polenta 41
cherries
    chocolate cherry tart 181
chia
    matcha chia pudding 34
    matcha strawberry chia pudding 34
    raspberry chia jam 21
chickpeas
    baked falafel 82
    chickpea cookie dough 174
    chuna mousse crostini 64
    chunky chickpea cookies 209
    curried chickpea jacket potatoes 115
    double chocolate chickpea balls 178
    pink beetroot hummus 52
    roasted garlic hummus 53

    spiced chickpeas 93
    sweet potato and capsicum soup 127
chilli
    chilli beans 140
    pico de gallo 140
chimichurri 41
chocolate
    apple cream bark 185
    chickpea cookie dough 174
    choc brownies with avocado frosting 214
    chocolate cherry tart 181
    double chocolate chickpea balls 178
    mint choc chip smoothie 45
    nutty caramel slice 182
    salted chocolate tahini fudge 193
chuna mousse crostini 64
chunky chickpea cookies 209
cinnamon
    cinnamon cream 201
    easy cinnamon scrolls 218
coconut
    brothy coconut noodles 163
    salted caramel and coconut protein balls 177
    raspberry ripe protein balls 179
coconut yoghurt
    coconut tzatziki 56
    peanut protein whip 25
    vanilla protein whip 30
cookie dough, chickpea 174
cookies, chunky chickpea 209
corn
    spiced corn and beans 94
couscous and sun-dried tomato salad 124
crackers, seeded 59
creams
    apple cream 185
    avocado crema 94
    cinnamon cream 201
    cream (cheat's tiramisu) 210
    cream (strawberry shortcake trifles) 213
    simple cashew cream 57
    spicy cashew cream 26

creamy dressing 86
creamy green pasta 143
crostini 64
croutons 90
crumble, raspberry 217
cucumber
    beetroot and cucumber bowl 78
    cucumber salad 78, 147
    Shirazi salad 82
curried chickpea jacket potatoes 115
curry
    curried chickpea jacket potatoes 115
    simple tofu curry 116
    Thai green curry 152

d
dates, Medjool
    miso date caramel smoothie 44
    roasted dates with pistachio butter 206
dhal, cheat's 159
dips
    butter bean and artichoke dip 55
    cashew queso 56
    chunky pesto 55
    coconut tzatziki 56
    pink beetroot hummus 52
    roasted garlic hummus 53
    spicy capsicum and walnut dip 54
dressing
    balsamic dressing 93
    Caesar dressing 90
    creamy dressing 86
    dressing (polenta caprese salad) 89
    sesame dressing 81

e
eggplant
    roasted eggplant with creamy slaw bowl 77

f
falafel
    baked falafel 82
    falafel mezze bowl 82
frittatas, pesto eggless 37
frosting 173
    avocado frosting 214
    cashew frosting 202

fudge, salted chocolate tahini 193

g
garlic
    garlic mushrooms 22
    garlicky potato soup 119
    roasted garlic hummus 53
gnocchi, marry me 151
gochujang
    gochujang sauce 147
    gochujang tofu burger 147
granola, oil-free 29
grilled satay skewers 63
guacamole 140

h
harissa
    whipped harissa tahini 77
hummus
    pink beetroot hummus 52
    roasted garlic hummus 53

i
iced desserts
    apple cream bark 185
    blueberry ice-cream bars 189
    mango matcha sorbet 190

j
jam
    raspberry chia jam 21
    raw strawberry jam 34

k
kale
    roasted veg on whipped tahini 128

l
lentils
    cheat's dhal 159
    easy lentil bolognaise 112
    mujadara inspired salad 111
    roasted veg on whipped tahini 128

m
mac and cheese, nut-free 160
mango
    creamy mango and pineapple smoothie 44
    mango matcha sorbet 190
    mango sorbet 190

marry me gnocchi 151
matcha
    mango matcha sorbet 190
    matcha sorbet 190
    matcha strawberry chia pudding 34
mini banoffee pies 186
mint choc chip smoothie 45
miso
    miso bean mash 156
    miso carrot pasta 120
    miso date caramel smoothie 44
    miso orange tofu 81
mocha hazelnut smoothie 43
mocha protein balls 176
mushrooms
    BBQ mushroom flatbreads 156
    BBQ mushrooms 156
    garlic mushrooms 22
mustardy potato salad 86

n
nachos, best (ever) vegan 140
nasi goreng, easy 148
noodles
    brothy coconut noodles 163
    carrot noodle soup 144
    orange and sesame noodle salad 81
    rainbow peanut noodles 155
nutty caramel slice 182

o
oats
    baked oats 30
    Bounty baked oats 30
    oil-free granola 29
    peanut butter and jam overnight oats 21
    snickez porridge 38
oil-free granola 29
olive oil
    spiced sweet potato and olive oil cake 202
onions
    mujadara inspired salad 111
    pickled onions 94
orange
    miso orange tofu 81
    orange and sesame noodle salad 81

p
pak choy 163
pan-fried broccolini and peas 97
pasta
    butternut pumpkin risoni 107
    creamy green pasta 143
    easy lentil bolognaise 112
    miso carrot pasta 120
    nut-free mac and cheese 160
peanut butter
    peanut butter and jam overnight oats 21
    peanut butter cookie protein balls 177
    peanut protein whip 25
    peanut sauce 155
    rainbow peanut noodles 155
peas
    pan-fried broccolini and peas 97
pesto
    chunky pesto 55
    pesto eggless frittatas 37
pickled onions 94
pico de gallo 140
pies, mini banoffee 186
pistachio butter 206
plums
    vanilla roasted plums with cinnamon cream 201
polenta 41
    baked polenta 89
    cheesy breakfast polenta 41
    polenta caprese salad 89
porridge, snickez 38
potatoes
    baked potato wedges with BBQ sauce 60
    curried chickpea jacket potatoes 115
    garlicky potato soup 119
    mustardy potato salad 86
    roasted potatoes 86
protein balls
    double chocolate chickpea balls 178
    mocha protein balls 176
    peanut butter cookie protein balls 177
    raspberry ripe protein balls 179

protein balls *continued*
   salted caramel and
     coconut protein balls 177
pumpkin
   butternut pumpkin
     risoni 107
   roasted veg on whipped
     tahini 128
   tray bake tacos 123

q
quinoa
   broccolini and crispy
     tempeh salad 97

r
rainbow peanut noodles 155
raspberries
   raspberry chia jam 21
   raspberry crumble 217
   raspberry ripe protein
     balls 179
rice
   black rice and rocket
     salad 93
   easy nasi goreng 148
   mujadara inspired
     salad 111
   simple tofu curry 116
   sweet potato and rice tray
     bake 108
risoni, butternut pumpkin 107
roasted carrots on whipped
   tofu 67
roasted cauliflower bowl 85
roasted dates with pistachio
   butter 206
roasted eggplant with creamy
   slaw bowl 77
roasted veg on whipped
   tahini 128
rocket
   black rice and rocket
     salad 93
   rocket salad 156
Romesco sauce 164

s
salads
   black rice and rocket
     salad 93
   broccolini and crispy
     tempeh salad 97
   butter bean Caesar 90
   cabbage slaw 77
   couscous and sun-dried

   tomato salad 124
   cucumber salad 78
   mujadara inspired
     salad 111
   mustardy potato salad 86
   orange and sesame noodle
     salad 81
   polenta caprese salad 89
   rocket salad 156
   Shirazi salad 82
   Tex Mex salad 94
salted caramel and coconut
   protein balls 177
salted chocolate tahini
   fudge 193
sandwich, cauliflower floret
   focaccia 164
satay
   grilled satay skewers 63
   satay sauce 63
sauces and condiments
   BBQ sauce 60
   capsicum sauce 85
   chimichurri 41
   gochujang sauce 147
   green sauce 143
   marry me sauce 151
   peanut sauce 155
   pico de gallo 140
   romanesco sauce 164
   satay sauce 63
   whipped harissa tahini 77
scrambled tofu 'eggs' 148
scrolls, easy cinnamon 218
seeded crackers 59
sesame
   orange and sesame noodle
     salad 81
   sesame dressing 81
simple cashew cream 57
simple tofu curry 116
slaw, cabbage 77
slice, nutty caramel 182
smoky baked beans 33
smoothies
   creamy mango and
     pineapple 44
   mint choc chip
     smoothie 45
   miso date caramel 44
   mocha hazelnut 43
   strawberries and cream 42
snickez porridge 38
soup
   brothy coconut
     noodles 163

   carrot noodle soup 144
   garlicky potato soup 119
   sweet potato and capsicum
     soup 127
spicy cashew cream 26
spicy tofu scramble breakfast
   tacos 26
spinach, wilted 41
strawberries
   matcha strawberry chia
     pudding 34
   raw strawberry jam 34
   strawberries and cream
     smoothie 42
   strawberry shortcake
     trifles 213
sweet potato
   roasted sweet potato 94
   spiced sweet potato and
     olive oil cake 202
   sweet potato and capsicum
     soup 127
   sweet potato and rice tray
     bake 108

t
tacos
   spicy tofu scramble
     breakfast tacos 26
   tray bake tacos 123
tahini
   roasted veg on whipped
     tahini 128
   salted chocolate tahini
     fudge 193
   tahini caramel 202
   whipped harissa tahini 77
tamari tofu 155
tart, chocolate cherry 181
tempeh
   broccolini and crispy
     tempeh salad 97
   crispy tempeh salad 97
Tex Mex salad 94
Thai green curry 152
tiramisu, cheat's 210
tofu
   gochujang tofu burger 147
   grilled satay skewers 63
   miso orange tofu 81
   roasted carrots on whipped
     tofu 67
   scrambled tofu 'eggs' 148
   simple tofu curry 116
   spicy tofu scramble
     breakfast tacos 26

   tamari tofu 155
   tofu scramble 26
   whipped tofu 67
tomatoes
   couscous and sun-dried
     tomato salad 124
   pico de gallo 140
   polenta caprese salad 89
   roasted vine tomatoes 41
   Shirazi salad 82
trifles, strawberry
   shortcake 213

v
vanilla coconut yoghurt
   peanut protein whip 25
   vanilla protein whip 30
vanilla roasted plums with
   cinnamon cream 201

w
walnuts
   spicy capsicum and walnut
     dip 54
wedges
   baked potato wedges with
     BBQ sauce 60
whipped harissa tahini 77
whipped tofu 67

PENGUIN BOOKS

UK | USA | Canada | Ireland | Australia
India | New Zealand | South Africa | China

Penguin Books is part of the Penguin Random House group of companies whose addresses can be found at global.penguinrandomhouse.com

First published by Penguin Books in 2024

Copyright © Chloe Wheatland in 2024

The moral right of the author has been asserted.

All rights reserved. No part of this publication may be reproduced, published, performed in public or communicated to the public in any form or by any means without prior written permission from Penguin Random House Australia Pty Ltd or its authorised licensees.

Cover and internal photography by Sammy Green
Food styling by Meryl Batlle
Cover and internal design by Kirby Armstrong
Typeset in Objektiv Mk1 and Source Serif Pro by Post Pre-press Group, Australia
Index by Puddingburn Publishing, Australia

Printed and bound in China by 1010 Printing International

 A catalogue record for this book is available from the National Library of Australia

ISBN 978 1 76134 899 0

penguin.com.au

We at Penguin Random House Australia acknowledge that Aboriginal and Torres Strait Islander peoples are the Traditional Custodians and the first storytellers of the lands on which we live and work. We honour Aboriginal and Torres Strait Islander peoples' continuous connection to Country, waters, skies and communities. We celebrate Aboriginal and Torres Strait Islander stories, traditions and living cultures; and we pay our respects to Elders past and present.